MODERN HINDI GRAMMAR

To the memory of Teddy–
who was always there

MODERN HINDI GRAMMAR

Stella Sandahl

LG PUBLISHERS DISTRIBUTORS

First Indian Edition 2015

ISBN 978-93-83723-07-2

₹ 295

Published by
LG PUBLISHERS DISTRIBUTORS
49, Lane No. 14, Pratap Nagar
Mayur Vihar Phase I, Delhi 110 091
Tel : 011 2279 5641 email: lgpdist@gmail.com

Printed at
Sapra Brothers, Delhi 110 092

INTRODUCTION.

The aim of this grammar is to present the Hindī language as clearly as possible in order to understand and translate correctly complex texts, both fiction and non-fiction. Its earliest *avatāra* – without the present chapter on syntax but with the practical alphabetical list of combined verbs – was written in Swedish in 1977 and used at Stockholm University and other Scandinavian universities. During my subsequent years of teaching Hindī at the University of Toronto, I constantly revised and hopefully improved it. Many of my Canadian students were sons and daughters of South Asian immigrants and therefore already knew how to speak Hindī and/or another modern Indo-Aryan language. To help them read sophisticated literary Hindī I devised a system of grammatical interpretation which I call syntagmatical analysis, a procedure which is described in the syntax part of this grammar. I have used certain terms which may seem idiosyncratic: for instance, 'combined verbs' instead of the usual term "compound verbs" (I reserve the latter term for the combination of nouns or adjectives with verbs). Moreover, I classify what is conventionally called the future tense as an aspectless presumptive within the subjunctive system. If my approach is unconventional, and hence suspect to some, my justification is that I know that it works on the practical level. An interesting side-effect of my method of analysing Hindī sentences was that students who later took Sanskrit with me could understand the grammatical structure of Sanskrit *samāsa*s (compounds) much more easily than students without such background.

This grammar is meant to be a reference grammar of the modern Hindī language written and spoken by educated speakers and taught in Hindī schools in the Hindī-speaking areas of India, i.e. Uttar Pradesh, Madhya Pradesh, Himachal Pradesh, Rajasthan and Bihar. Of course there are differences both in pronunciation and in intonation over such a vast area, but these differences are not an obstacle to mutual understanding. The written language may also show some dialectal differences, especially when dialect is deliberately used for literary purposes. These variations are stylistic and are not discussed in the present grammar. The sentence structure is the same over the entire area.

What is Modern Standard Hindī? It is generally agreed that its base is *khaṛī bolī*, the dialect of the Delhi-Meruth area. *Khaṛī bolī* is an Indo-Aryan language which ultimately descends from Sanskrit, or, more precisely, from one of the spoken Sanskrit dialects of which no written records survive. Its structure is Indo-Aryan, and the bulk of its vocabulary derived from Sanskrit. I shall use the conventional term *tadbhav* "of the nature of that" (i.e. of Sanskrit) throughout this grammar. Most verbs and pronouns in modern Hindī are *tadbhav*. However, it should not be forgotten that Delhi was the capital of Muslim India, and that the court language of the Muslim rulers of India was originally Persian. Hence, over the course of time a "language of contact" developed, called Urdū, which is short for *zabān-e-urdū*, "the language of the camp". Urdū enriched the *tadbhav* vocabulary of *kharī bolī* with a vast number of nouns, a few verbs and one reflexive pronoun, but the sentence structure remained Indo-Aryan. For words of Persian, Arabic or even Turkish origin I shall use the conventional term *videśī* "foreign" in this grammar, although its implications are somewhat misleading. Hindī and Urdū are essentially the same language, born of the same soil. The same term *videśī* is also applied to vocabulary taken over from English, Portuguese, French, and so forth.

Videśī is the opposite of *deśī*, "of the country, indigenous", a word which is applied both to dialectal words borrowed from within the Indo-Aryan linguistic area and to words of Dravidian and Munda origin.

The term *tatsam* literally means "same as that", i.e. same as Sanskrit. This term operates on two levels: it was obviously natural to preserve Sanskrit terms in the religious and liturgical vocabulary of Hinduism and in learned discourse about Sanskrit literature, classical Indian philosophy, astrology and so forth. The other use of *tatsam* words is a recent phenomenon: there is an ongoing coinage of "new" *tatsam* words in the language in the fields of administration and the sciences, in radio and television in an effort to Sanskritize the vocabulary. However, these neologisms are not really *tatsam*, since the reality they correspond to is a contemporary one. Thus we have *dūrdarśan* for "television" – literally meaning "seeing far", *dūrbhāṣ* for "telephone", *ākāśvāṇī* for "radio", *pradhān mantrī* for "prime minister". Many of these "new" *tatsam* coinages have established themselves, but some died of ridicule – for instance, the infamous *agnirathavirāmasthāna* "the stopping-place for the fire chariot" intended to replace the *videśī* term *sṭeśan* for "railway station".

However, as the Kabīr dictum goes, *bhāṣā caltī nadī* "language [is] a flowing river": the Hindī language will continue to follow its own course of change. The river is bound to change – the goal of a grammar is not to create a pool of stagnant water. The present grammar describes the river at a certain time, at a certain point. Although it is bound to be washed away sooner or later by the continuous process of linguistic change, it may help students of Hindī today to come to grips with a wonderful rich language whose comprehension is the only means to a full understanding of the rich and varied culture of North India.

Stella Sandahl
Toronto 1999

TABLE OF CONTENTS

SCRIPT AND PRONUNCIATION.

§ 1. The devanāgarī script used for Standard Hindī is a phonetic script inherited from Sanskrit. Correct pronunciation can only be achieved through hearing and repeating phonetic exercise tapes in a language laboratory or through exercises with a teacher who is a native speaker. Since English has a tendency to diphthongize vowels, I have preferred not to give approximate English equivalents which in the end are bound to be misleading. Consonants are by and large similar to English consonants with a few exceptions noted below. Here follows a phonetic descriptions of the sounds, giving the nāgarī script sign, the standard transliteration and, when required, the IPA symbol.

PHONETICS AND PHONOLOGY.

§ 2. VOWELS.

Hindī has ten vowel phonemes: अ a, आ ā, इ i, ई ī, उ u, ऊ ū, ए e, ऐ ai (IPA æ), ओ o, and औ au (IPA ɔ).

TABLE

		Front unrounded	Mid unrounded	Back unrounded	rounded
Closed	High	ई ī इ i			ऊ ū उ u
Halfclosed Halfopen	Middle	ए e ऐ ai /æ/	 अ a	 औ au /ɔ/	ओ o
Open	Low			आ ā	

§ 3. Quantity: Traditional Indian grammar distinguishes between short and long vowels. However, in the cases of इ/ई i/ī and उ/ऊ u/ū the difference lies rather in the degree of tension. That a tense vowel tends to be perceived as longer than a lax vowel is a secondary phenomenon. Regarding अ/आ a/ā, the difference lies in the quality rather than the quantity.

§ 4. Degrees of tension:

Very tense:	ई ī	ऊ ū	
Tense:	आ ā	ए e	ओ o
Halftense:	ऐ ai /æ/	औ au /ɔ/	
Lax:	अ a	इ i	उ u

§ 5. Length of vowels:

Short:	अ a	इ i	उ u				
Long:	आ ā	ई ī	ऊ ū	ए e	ओ o	ऐ ai	औ au

§ 6. The distinction between short and long vowels (or tense and lax vowels) has a phonemic as well as prosodic value. In the normal spoken language, however, long vowels often become half-long or even short in unstressed positions. आ /ā/ in जा *jā* "go!" is obviously longer than the same आ /ā/ in जाएगा *jāegā* "he will go", since the stress in जाएगा *jāegā* falls on ए /e/.

§ 7. In the nominal and verbal paradigms, ई /-ī-/ and ऊ /-ū-/ are shortened before stressed long vowels of endings. This is reflected in the spelling also. Between shortened इ /-i-/ and the following vowel the glide य -y- is often inserted (see §§ 34, 37).

§ 8. Pronunciation of vowels (in alphabetical order):

अ a is a short half-open unrounded lax mid central vowel.
आ ā is a long open tense mid-back vowel
इ i is a short closed lax unrounded high front vowel.
ई ī is a long closed tense unrounded high front vowel.
उ u is a short closed lax rounded high back vowel.

ऊ ū is a long closed tense rounded high back vowel.

ऋ ṛ, pronounced /ri/ or sometimes /ru/, is classified as a vowel in traditional grammars and in dictionaries. However, it ceased to be an independent vowel already during the High Middle Indo-Aryan period (it does not occur in Pālī). It is kept in Hindī dictionaries because *tatsam* words maintain the Sanskrit spelling, i.e. ऋण *ṛṇ*, pronounced रिण *riṇ* "debt", ऋषि *ṛṣi*, pronounced रिषि *riṣi* "sage".

ए e is a long closed tense unrounded mid-back vowel.

ऐ ai, pronounced /æ/ is a long, half-open, half-tense low front vowel.

ओ o is a long, half-closed, tense, rounded mid-back vowel.

औ au, pronounced as a half-open less tense version of the preceding /o/, IPA /ɔ/.

Note that ऐ ai and औ au are **not** diphthongs in MSH.

§ 9. The vowel-signs depicted above occur only in initial position or following another vowel. Vowels immediately following consonants have the following shapes:

अ	short /a/ is always inherent in the unmodified consonant letter:	क	ka
आ	is reduced to ा	का	kā
इ	is reduced to ि and placed **before** the consonant:	कि	ki
ई	is reduced to ी and placed after the consonant:	की	kī
उ	is reduced to ु and placed under the consonant: Exception रु ru.	कु	ku
ऊ	is reduced to ू and placed under the consonant: Exception रू rū.	कू	kū
ऋ	is reduced to ृ and placed under the consonant:	कृ	kṛ
ए	is reduced to े and placed on top of the consonant:	के	ke
ऐ	is reduced to ै and placed on top of the consonant:	कै	kai
ओ	is reduced to ो and placed after the consonant: (Learn to distinguish between ी ī and ो o: गी gī – गो go)	को	ko
औ	is reduced to ौ and placed after the consonant:	कौ	kau

§ 10. The phonemic status of all vowels can be established through contrast:

कटना	*kaṭnā*	"to be cut"	काटना	*kāṭnā*	"to cut"
कि	*ki*	"that"	की	*kī*	(fem. gen.-marker)
कुल	*kul*	"family"	कूल	*kūl*	"shore"
बेल	*bel*	"bel" (a kind of fruit)	बैल	*bail*	"ox"
ओर	*or*	"direction"	और	*aur*	"and"

§ 11. Nasalization. All vowels can be nasalized and contrasted to the corresponding unnasalized version. The nasal is either written as a superscript ˙ called अनुस्वार *anusvār* or as ँ called चन्द्रबिन्दु *candrabindu* or अनुनासिक *anunāsik*. Theoretically, a nasalized vowel should be indicated by a *candrabindu*, but it is practically impossible to write a *candrabindu* after superscript reduced vowelsigns such as ि, ी, े, ै, ो, ौ, so the simple *anusvār* sign has to be used: for example कीं, कें, कों, कौं.

कथा	*kathā*	"story"	कँथा	*kãthā*	"a patch-work garment"
कहा	*kahā*	"said"	कहाँ	*kahã*	"where?"
इधर	*idhar*	"over here"	इँधन	*ĩdhan*	"fuel"
चली	*calī*	"she went"	चलीं	*calī̃*	"they (fem.) went"
भूसा	*bhūsā*	"straw"	भूँसा	*bhū̃sā*	"barked" (p. p.)
बेटा	*beṭā*	"son"	बेंट	*bẽṭ*	"handle"
है	*hai*	"is"	हैं	*hãi*	"are"
लड़को	*laṛko*	"boys!" (voc. pl.)	लड़कों	*laṛkõ*	"boys" (obl. pl.)
कौन	*kaun*	"who?"	कौंधना	*kãudhnā*	"to glitter"

§ 12. Qualitative variants of vowel phonemes.

1. Unstressed अ /a/ is pronounced as schwa /ʌ /: सड़क *saṛak* "street" /saṛʌk/.

2. अ /a/ before ह /ha/ in a stressed syllable is pronounced /æ /: कहना *kahnā* "to say" is pronounced /kænā/, /kæhnā/ or /kæhænā/. In an unstressed syllable the pronunciation of अ /a/ reverts to ordinary /a/: कहा /kahā/, रहेगा /rahegā/.

3. In a few feminine nouns final -ah may be pronounced /e/ or /eh/: तरह *tarah* is pronounced /tare/, /tareh/ or, regularly /taræh/.

4. In the numerals 11-18 final -ah is pronounced as अ /a/ or आ /ā/: सोलह *solah* "sixteen" /sola/ or /solā/, ग्यारह *gyārah* "eleven" /gyāra/ or /gyārā/.

5. Note the pronunciation of final -ah in the pronoun यह *yah* "this": /yæh/, /yæhæ / or /yi/ .

6. The pronoun वह *vah* "that" is normally pronounced /vɔ /. However, some Hindī schoolteachers insist that *vah* should be pronounced as / væhæ / especially when reading aloud.

7. Final -ay may be pronounced /-ay/, /æ/, /ae/ or /æe/. This sound group is most common in *tatsam* words, e.g. समय *samay* "time".

8. In *videśī* words an unstressed short -अ- can be realized as /ʌ /, /a/, /i/ or /u/: मुस्कराना /muskʌrānā/, /muskirānā/ or /muskurānā/ "to smile", बाहर /bāhar/ or /bāhir/ "outside".

9. Consonant-groups are often dissolved through an unstressed inserted vowel, which may be realized as /a/, /ʌ/, /i/ or /u/: गर्म *garm* "hot" is pronounced /garʌm/ or /garam/, बर्फ़ *barf* "snow, ice" as /barʌf/ or /baraf/, ब्रुश *bruś* "brush" as /buruʃ/, ग्लास *glās* "glass" as /gilās/. The spelling is often adjusted according to actual pronunciation, since the devanāgarī script is a phonetic script: गरम, बरफ़, बुरुश, गिलास.

10. The inherent /a/ in final consonant-clusters is realized as a schwa: विश्व /viśvʌ /, पत्र /patrʌ /.

§ **13.** Consonants.

Hindī consonants reflect the history of the Hindī language. Thus Hindī has thirty three *tatsam* consonants, of which there are twenty stops or plosives, subdivided into unvoiced and voiced, unaspirated and aspirated, five homorganic nasals, four "semivowels", three unvoiced sibilants, and a voiced glottal fricative. There are also two *tadbhav* retroflex flaps: ṛ and ṛh and *videśī* consonants, which occur only in words of Arabic, Persian, English and other origin and can be regarded as variants of indigenous *tatsam* consonants, i.e. they have no phonemic value with the possible exception of /z/. The variants will be discussed below along with the corresponding *tatsam* consonants.

§ **14.** A short अ /a/ is inherent in every consonant which does not show another vowelsign.

§ 15. Phonetic inventory.

Unvoiced unaspirated stops:	ka क	ca च	ṭa ट	ta त	pa प
	qa क़				
Unvoiced aspirated stops:	kha ख	cha छ	ṭha ठ	tha थ	pha फ
Voiced unaspirated stops:	ga ग	ja ज	ḍa ड	da द	ba ब
Voiced aspirated stops:	gha घ	jha झ	ḍha ढ	dha ध	bha भ
Nasals:	ṅa ङ	ña ञ	ṇa ण	na न	ma म
Semivowels:	ya य			va व	
Voiced alveolars or laterals:	ra र	la ल			
Unvoiced fricatives:	k̲h̲a (xa) ख़	śa श	ṣa ष	sa स	fa फ़
Voiced fricatives:	ha ह	ġa (γa) ग़		za ज़	
Unaspirated retroflex flap:	ṛa ड़				
Aspirated retroflex flap:	ṛha ढ़				
Voiced aspiration:	ḥ :				

§ 16. From the point of articulation the sounds are divided as follows (variants are indicated in paranthesis).

	Stops		Fricatives	
	Unvoiced	Voiced	Unvoiced	Voiced
Laryngeal				ह
Uvular	(क़)		(ख़)	(ग़)
Velar	क ख	ग घ		
Front palatal or Pre-palatal affricates	च छ	ज झ	श	

Palato-alveolar						(ज़)
Retroflex	ट	ठ	ड	ढ	(ष)	
Dental	त	थ	द	ध	स	(ज़)
Labio-dental					(फ़)	
Bilabial	प	फ	ब	भ		
Voiced aspiration						(:)

	Nasals	Lateral	Flaps	Semivowels
Velar	(ङ)			
Front palatal	(ञ)			य
Retroflex	(ण)		ड़ ढ़	
Alveolar or Post-dental		ल		र
Dental	न			
Labio-dental				व
Bilabial	म			

§ 17. All nasals, laterals, flaps and semi-vowels are voiced.

§ 18. Description of individual sounds following the devanāgarī alphabetical order with transliteration:

क *ka* is an unvoiced velar stop as in काका *kākā* "uncle".
Its variant क़ *qa* is an unvoiced uvular stop which occurs in Arabic and Persian loanwords: क़लम *qalam* "pen".
क़ *qa* is used mainly by Urdū-speakers. MSH prefers *ka*.

ख *kha* is an unvoiced aspirated velar stop as in खाना *khānā* "to eat".
Its variant ख़ *kha/xa* is an unvoiced uvular fricative used in AP loanwords: ख़बर *xabar* "news", अख़बार *axbār* "newspaper". It is regularly used in Urdū, and sometimes in MSH.

ग *ga* is a voiced velar stop as in गाना *gānā* "song". AP loanwords have the variant ग़ *ga* (ɣa) which is a voiced uvular fricative: ग़रीब *garīb* "poor". It is only used by Urdū-speakers. MSH prefers the pronunciation *ga:garīb*.

घ *gha* is a voiced aspirated velar stop: घर *ghar* "house".

ङ *ṅa* is the velar homorganic nasal. It can only appear before velar stops, thus excluding its appearance in initial position: आङ्ख *āṅkh* "eye". See § 21 below.

च *ca* is listed as an unvoiced palatal stop in most grammars. It is, however, rather a pre-palatal affricate: चलना *calnā* "to go".

छ *cha* is the aspirated version of the previous *ca* , i.e. an aspirated unvoiced pre-palatal affricate: छलना *chalnā* "to deceive".

ज *ja* is a voiced pre-palatal affricate: जाना *jānā* "to go". It has the variant ज़ /za/, a voiced fricative, articulated either as a palato-alveolar or a dental, found in *videśī* words such as बाज़ार *bāzār* "market", ज़रूर *zarūr* "certainly". Dental ज़ /za/ can be opposed to the unvoiced dental fricative स /sa/: प्यास *pyās* "thirst")(प्याज़ *pyāz* "onion".
However, this does not make ज़ /za/ a phoneme, since many speakers will pronounce प्याज़ as प्याज *pyāj* .

झ *jha* is an aspirated voiced pre-palatal affricate: झट *jhaṭ* "at once"

ञ *ña* is the palatal homorganic nasal, found before palatal stops (= prepalatal affricates): जाञ्च *jāñc* "investigation". It cannot appear in initial position. See § 21 below.

ट *ṭa* is an unvoiced retroflex stop, pronounced with the tip of the tongue towards the upper palate: मोटा "fat". It is phonemically distinct from the dental त /ta/. See § 20 below.

ठ *ṭha* is the aspirated unvoiced retroflex: ठाकुर *ṭhākur* "lord, master".

ड *ḍa* is the voiced retroflex stop: डाह *ḍāh* "jealousy, envy".

ड़ *ṛa* is a retroflex flap. It cannot occur initially. Phonemically, it is a variant of the voiced retroflex stop, occuring in *tadbhav* words: पड़ना *paṛnā* "to fall" (< Skt. √ *pat*, with Pkt. retroflexion of dental consonants).

ढ *ḍha* is an aspirated voiced retroflex: ढंग *ḍhaṅg* "manner, mode".

ढ़ *ṛha* is an aspirated retroflex flap. Like ड़ it cannot occur initially, and may be considered a variant of the aspirated voiced retroflex stop. It occurs in *tadbhav* words: पढ़ना *paṛhnā* "to read" (< Skt. √ *paṭh*).

ण *ṇa* is the homorganic retroflex nasal. It cannot occur initially. Intervocalically it occurs only in *tatsam* words such as गणित *gaṇit* "mathematics", गणिका *gaṇikā* "courtesan, prostitute". Its phonemic value can be disputed, see § 21 below.

त *ta* is an unvoiced dental stop: तागा *tāgā* "thread". See § 20 below.

थ *tha* is an aspirated unvoiced dental stop: थाना *thānā* "police-station".

द *da* is a voiced dental stop: दल *dal* "party".

ध *dha* is an aspirated voiced dental stop: धूप *dhūp* "sunshine"

न *na* is a dental nasal. It can occur in initial, intervocalic and final position: नम *nam* "humid", लाना *lānā* "to bring", मन *man* "mind, heart". It is a nasal phoneme opposed to the bilabial nasal /*m*/. See § 21 below.

प *pa* is an unvoiced bilabial stop: पागल *pāgal* "mad, crazy"

फ *pha* is an aspirated unvoiced bilabial stop: फल *phal* "fruit". It has as variant the unvoiced labio-dental fricative फ़ *fa* found in *videsī* words: फ़िल्म *film* "film", फ़र्क *fark* "difference".

ब *ba* is the voiced bilabial stop: बिल्ली *billī* "cat".

भ *bha* is the aspirated voiced bilabial stop: भालू *bhālū* "bear"

म *ma* is the bilabial nasal: मदद *madad* "help". See § 21 below.

य *ya* is a front palatal semivowel: यदि *yadi* "if".

र *ra* is a voiced alveolar or post-dental with a weak flap: रात rāt "night", रोग *rog* "illness".

ल *la* is a voiced alveolar or post-dental lateral, phonemically opposed to the preceding र *ra*: लात *lāt* "kick", लोग *log* "people".

व *va* is a labio-dental semivowel: वन *van* "forest".

श *śa* is an unvoiced front palatal fricative: शरीर *śarīr* "body".

ष *ṣa* is an unvoiced retroflex fricative. Its pronunciation does not differ from the preceding front palatal fricative श *śa*. ष is found only in *tatsam* words: विष्णु *Viṣṇu* Vishnu, कृष्ण *kṛṣṇa* Krishna, ऋषि (pronounced रिषि – see § 8) "sage".

स *sa* is a dental fricative, phonemically opposed to the two precedent fricatives: शिला *śilā* "rock")(सिला *silā* "stitched".

ह *ha* is a voiced laryngal fricative: होना *honā* "to be".

: *ḥa* is a voiced aspiration, called विसर्ग *visarg*, present only in *tatsam* words. It cannot appear in initial position, has no phonemic value, and is mostly left unpronounced in MSH. It is often deleted even in the spelling: दुःख *duḥkh* or दुख *dukh* "sorrow".

§ 19. Aspiration is a salient feature of Hindī phonology: aspirated stops are always phonemically opposed to unaspirated stops:

काई	*kāī*	"moss"	खाई	*khāī*	"trench, moat"
गिरना	*girnā*	"to fall"	घिरना	*ghirnā*	"to be surrounded"
चलना	*calnā*	"to go"	छलना	*chalnā*	"to deceive"
जूठा	*jūṭhā*	"defiled"	झूठा	*jhūṭhā*	"false"
टीका	*ṭīkā*	"vaccination"	ठीका also ठेका	*ṭhīkā/ṭhekā*	"contract"
डाक	*ḍāk*	"mail, post"	ढाक	*ḍhāk*	"flame-of-the forest" (a tree)
पड़ना	*paṛnā*	"to fall"	पढ़ना	*paṛhnā*	"to read"
ताना	*tānā*	"taunt"	थाना	*thānā*	"police-station"
दावा	*dāvā*	"claim, suit"	धावा	*dhāvā*	"raid, attack"
पल	*pal*	"instant"	फल	*phal*	"fruit"
बला	*balā*	"calamity"	भला	*bhalā*	"good"

§ 20. There is a phonemic distinction between retroflex and dental stops in Hindī. Compare the following pairs:

मोटी	*moṭī*	"fat" (fem.adj.)	मोती	*motī*	"pearl"
ठानना	*ṭhānnā*	"to resolve"	तानना	*tānnā*	"to stretch"
डाल	*ḍāl*	"branch"	दाल	*dāl*	"lentil"
ढाक	*ḍhāk*	"flame-of-the-forest"	धाक	*dhāk*	"sway, awe"

The English alveolar stops /t/ and /d/ are perceived as retroflex in Hindī and rendered as such in the devanāgarī script: स्टेशन *sṭeśan* "railway station", डाक्टर *ḍākṭar* "doctor".

§ 21. Of the five nasal sounds in Hindī, only n *na* and m *ma* can be said to have phonemic status. The velar and the palatal nasals, ङ *ṅa* and ञ *ña* can only appear before sounds of the same group, for example अङ्ग *aṅg* "member", चञ्चल *cañcal* "unsteady", never in initial and intervocalic positions.

Although the retroflex nasal ण *ṇa* can appear alone intervocalically it does so only in *tatsam* words such as in गणित *gaṇit* "mathematics". It cannot be contrasted with any other nasal, and can never appear in initial position. Consequently, it seems justified to say that ङ, ञ and ण *(ṅa, ña* and *ṇa)* are all variants of न *na* . The bilabial nasal म *ma* is an independent phoneme which can be contrasted with न as in नाना *nānā* "maternal grandfather" as opposed to मामा *māmā* "maternal uncle".

§ 22. All homorganic nasals may be – and often are – replaced by the superscript sign ˙ called *anusvār* (see § 11 above) : अङ्क is written अंक *ãk*, अञ्चल is written अंचल *ãcal*, दण्ड is written दंड *dãḍ*, दान्त as दांत *dãt*, लम्बा as लंबा *lãbā*.

§ 23. As stated above (§ 14), short अ /a/ is inherent in every consonant which does not show another vowel-sign. However, in certain phonetic contexts the inherent /a/ is not pronounced at all. These contexts are:

1. in final position: कमल *kamal* "lotus", पागल *pāgal* "crazy".

2. in words containing three consonants if an inherent /a/ is followed by a consonant containing a vowel other than /a/: गमला *gamlā* "flower-pot", गलती *galtī* "mistake", करना *karnā* "to do", देखना *dekhnā* "to see" (most infinitives fall into this category).

3. in words containing four consonants the inherent /a/ is not pronounced in the ante-paenultimate consonant: बकबक *bakbak* "prattle", मनसूबा *mansūbā* " plan, design", मदहोश *madhoś* "dead drunk".

4. Some *videśī* words of Persian or Arabic origin do not always follow the rules above: अजनबी *ajnabī* "stranger" (and not *ajanbī*), आमदनी *āmadnī* "revenue".

CONJUNCT CONSONANTS.

§ 24. Since all consonants contain an inherent /a/ there is a procedure to delete it by appending a short stroke below the consonant sign: क् /k/ . This is called विराम *virām* "cessation".

§ 25. The inherent अ /a/ must disappear in consonant clusters too. The way to make conjunct consonants is simple: only the last consonant in the cluster is written out in full, the preceding ones are treated in different ways:

1. By reducing the first consonant: क्क kka, क्य kya, ग्य gya.
2. By superposition (this is often done with the velar and palatal homorganic nasals):
   ङ्क ṅka, ङ्ख ṅkha, ङ्ग ṅga, ङ्घ ṅgha, ञ्च ñca, ञ्ज ñja,
   ट्ट ṭṭa, द्ग dga, द्व dva, द्भ dbha etc.
3. Conjunct consonants with /r/ are treated in special ways:
   a. If /r/ is following the consonant it is realised as ् under the letter: प्र pra ब्र bra क्र kra etc. However त + र has the special sign त्र.
   b. If /r/ precedes the consonant it is realised as ॅ on top of the line: र्क rka र्प rpa र्भ rbha र्ह rha, etc. If this group is followed by a long vowel the /r/ sign comes after the vowel: र्ती rtī, र्भे rbhe, अर्थात *arthāt* "namely".
   Regarding रु and रू see § 9.
4. A few conjunct consonants have special shapes: क्ष kṣa, क्त kta (also regularly क्त), ज्ञ jña, त्त tta, त्र tra, द्य dya, and श्र śra.
5. Conjunct consonants beginning with ह /ha/ appear as
   ह्र hra, ह्ण hṇa, ह्ल hla, ह्न hna, ह्म hma, ह्व hva.

STRESS, ACCENT AND INTONATION.

§ 26. Hindī has a level syllabic stress. The general tendency is to stress long vowels somewhat more than short ones in isolated words, and to mark the end syllable of a syntagmatic unit with a short pause (see § 459). Hindī does **not** have an emphatic stress – emphasis is made through emphatic particles (see §§ 439-442) and/or inversion of the normal word-order (see §§ 464, 469).

§ 27. In isolated words Hindī has a light stress in syllables with short vowels, i.e. अ, इ, उ : बस *bas* "enough!", दिल *dil* "heart", कुछ *kuch* "some".

§ 28. In polysyllabic words with short vowels a slightly more marked stress falls on the first syllable: कमल *kamal* "lotus", नगर *nagar* "city", किधर *kidhar* "where?". However, if the first syllable is a prefix, the accent may fall on the first syllable after the prefix: प्रगति *pragati* "progress", निकलना *nikalnā* "to emerge", परितुष्ट *parituṣṭ* "gratified".

§ 29. Long vowels, i.e. आ, ई, ऊ, ए, ऐ, ओ and औ are always stressed: प्रजा *prajā* "people", ख़ुशी *xuśī / khuśī* "joy", जादू *jādū* "magic", खेती *khetī* "agriculture", धोबी *dhobī* "washerman", रोटी *roṭī* "bread", खिलौना *khilaunā* "toy".

§ 30. A short vowel followed by two consonants counts as a heavy syllable and is stressed: उल्लू *ullū* "owl, fool" इन्हें *inhẽ* "them".

§ 31. Double consonants are phonemically different from single consonants:

उसे	*use*	"[to] him/her"	उस से	*us se*	"from him/her"
पता	*patā*	"address"	पत्ता	*pattā*	"leaf"
पटा	*paṭā*	"scimitar"	पट्टा	*paṭṭā*	"deed, lease"

NOUNS.

§ 32. The Hindī noun has

A. two genders: masculine and feminine.
B. two numbers: singular and plural.
C. three cases: direct, oblique and vocative
D. four declensions: 1. masculines in -आ and -आँ
2. feminines in -ई and -इ
3. other masculines
4. other feminines.

DECLENSION: TABLES

§ 33. **1st declension** – masculine nouns in -आ and -आँ:
बेटा "son", कुआँ "well"

	Sg.		Pl.	
Dir.	बेटा	कुआँ	बेटे	कुएँ
Obl.	बेटे	कुएँ	बेटों	कुओं
Voc.	बेटा, बेटे	कुएँ	बेटो	कुओं

Note that the nasalization in कुआँ is maintained all through the paradigm.

§ 34. **2nd declension** – feminine nouns in -ई and -इ:
बेटी "daughter", विधि "law, method"

	Sg.		Pl.	
Dir.	बेटी	विधि	बेटियाँ	विधियाँ
Obl.	बेटी	विधि	बेटियों	विधियों
Voc.	बेटी	विधि	बेटियो	विधियो

Note that in all three cases of the plural, -ई is shortened since the endings are long, stressed vowels, i.e. -आँ, -ओं and -ओ, and the glide -य- is inserted. Cf. § 37.

§ 35. Feminine nouns ending in -इया (usually diminutives) form the plural by nasalizing the final vowel, thus following the 2nd declension: चिड़िया "bird", डिब्बिया "little box"

	Sg.		Pl.	
Dir.	चिड़िया	डिब्बिया	चिड़ियाँ	डिब्बियाँ
Obl.	चिड़िया	डिब्बिया	चिड़ियों	डिब्बियों
Voc.	चिड़िया	डिब्बिया	चिड़ियो	डिब्बियो

§ 36. **3rd declension** – all other masculine nouns: किसान "peasant"

	Sg.	Pl.
Dir.	किसान	किसान
Obl.	किसान	किसानों
Voc.	किसान	किसानो

§ 37. Masculine nouns ending in -ई and -ऊ shorten the stem vowel before the stressed long vowels in the obl. and voc. pl. Stems in -ई also insert the glide -य- before the ending (cf. § 34 above): आदमी "man", भालू "bear"

	Sg.		Pl.	
Dir.	आदमी	भालू	आदमी	भालू
Obl.	आदमी	भालू	आदमियों	भालुओं
Voc.	आदमी	भालू	आदमियो	भालुओ

§ 38. Some masculines in -आ follow the 3rd declension, **not** the 1st. They are as follows:

1. *tatsam* nouns in -आ :
   राजा "king", पिता "father", नेता "leader"

	Sg.			Pl.		
Dir.	राजा	पिता	नेता	राजा	पिता	नेता
Obl.	राजा	पिता	नेता	राजाओं	पिताओं	नेताओं
Voc.	राजा	पिता	नेता	राजाओ	पिताओ	नेताओ
	राजन्					

Note: the alternative voc. sg. राजन् is the Skt. form.

2. masculine kinship terms in -आ: दादा "paternal grandfather", नाना "maternal grandfather", चाचा "paternal uncle" , मामा "maternal uncle", etc.

3. some *videśī* nouns of Persian-Arabic origin: ख़ुदा "God", सूरमा "hero", दारोग़ा "sub-inspector (of police)"

§ 39. **4th declension** – all other feminine nouns: बहिन "sister"

	Sg.	Pl.
Dir.	बहिन	बहिनें
Obl.	बहिन	बहिनों
Voc.	बहिन	बहिनो

§ 40. In a few isolated cases feminine nouns of the 2nd declension may be conjugated according to the 4th declension in **dir. pl**: सीढ़िएँ "stairs" instead of सीढ़ियाँ (from sg. सीढ़ी "stair"). Cf. § 62.2.

GENDER.

§ 41. All Hindī nouns are either masculine or feminine. The gender is of course arbitrary except in cases of obvious natural gender, i.e. words implying "man" are masculine, words implying "woman" are feminine. The gender of a particular noun, however, often reflects its historical origin: with a few exceptions *tatsam* and *tadbhav* nouns usually keep the gender they had in Sanskrit, where gender was also arbitrary. The Sanskrit neuter has merged with the masculine in Hindī. *videśī* nouns entered the Hindī language later through political conquest and/or social contact: these, which are mainly of Persian, Arabic or English origin, have acquired a gender in Hindī through usage and their form has whenever necessary been phonetically adjusted to the general pattern of Hindī nouns.

§ 42. As can be seen from the declension tables (§§ 33, 34), nouns ending in -ई, -आ -ā and -आँ -ā are usually masculine and nouns ending in -ī are usually feminine. Most of these are *tadbhav* nouns.

लड़का	"boy"	लड़की	"girl"
बेटा	"son"	बेटी	"daughter"
घोड़ा	"horse"	घोड़ी	"mare"

Note that in the last example घोड़ा masc. is the general word for horse, male or female, whereas the fem. घोड़ी specifically refers to a mare. In the case of

बिल्ली *billī* fem. "cat", the feminine is the general term. The masc. बिल्ला means "tom cat". In the case of भेड़ा masc. "ram" and भेड़ी fem. "ewe", the general term is भेड़ fem. "sheep".

§ 43. When words are paired in masc. –आ and fem. –ई stems, the feminine often has a diminutive meaning:

रस्सा	"rope"	रस्सी	"string"
पत्ता	"leaf"	पत्ती	"small leaf"
कटोरा	"bowl"	कटोरी	"small bowl"

Note however:

घड़ा	"pot, pitcher"	घड़ी	"watch"

§ 44. Masculine nouns ending in –आ .

1. –आ is the normal *tadbhav* ending for masculine nouns and provides the paradigm for the 1st declension (see § 33).
2. The masculine *tatsam* in –आ follow the 3rd declension (see §§ 36, 38.1). They represent the nom. sing. of Sanskrit masculine stems in –तृ or masculine and neuter stems in –अन् : पिता "father", नेता "leader", दाता "giver", राजा "king", आत्मा "soul".
3. Many *videśī* nouns from Arabic or Persian have been adjusted to the pattern of the 1st declension, e.g. masculine nouns in –आ (§ 33): दरिया "river, दर्ज़ा "class, rank", कारख़ाना "factory". A few masculine *videśī* nouns follow the 3rd declension (see § 38.3).

§ 45. Feminine nouns in –आ :

1. The feminine *tatsam* usually represent either the nominative singular of Sanskrit feminine stems in –आ such as कन्या "virgin", इच्छा "wish, desire", अहिंसा "non-violence", or the nom. sing. in –ता of feminine stems in –तृ such as माता "mother", दुहिता "daughter".
2. *tatsam* abstract nouns in –ता : दरिद्रता "poverty", धूर्तता "crookednesss".
3. *neo-tatsam* fem. nouns such as लेखिका "authoress" from masc. लेखक "author", अध्यापिका "teacher, school-mistress".
4. some *videśī* feminines such as दुनिया *duniyā* "world", हवा *havā* "air", दवा *davā* "medicine", बला *balā* "calamity".

All the above categories follow the 4th declension (see § 39).

§ 46. Nouns ending in -इया are usually feminine and often diminutives (see § 35). However, there are masculine nouns in -इया, mostly referring to animate beings, thus displaying natural gender: डाकिया "postman", गवैया "singer". -इया may also have a pejorative meaning when applied to masculine nouns: सिपाहिया "cop".

§ 47. Nouns in -इ.

1. Most nouns ending in -इ- are *tatsam* feminines abstract nouns: मुक्ति "salvation", भक्ति "devotion", शक्ति "strength, energy", आपत्ति "objection", विपत्ति "affliction", विधि "law, method", ध्वनि "sound" (the last two are masc. in Sanskrit, and they were masc. in 19th century Hindī) .
2. There is a small number of masculine *tatsam* nouns in -इ-: अतिथि "guest", कपि "monkey", रवि "sun". The general tendency, however, is for most *tatsam* words in -इ- which were masc. or neuter in Sanskrit to become feminine in modern Hindī (such as विधि and ध्वनि listed above).

§ 48. Nouns in -ई.

1. -ई is the normal *tadbhav* feminine declension ending and provides the paradigm for the 2nd declension (see § 34).
2. Abstract nouns derived from Arabic or Persian adjectives are feminine: खुशी "happiness", बेशर्मी "shamelessness", गरीबी "poverty", ज़बरदस्ती "highhandedness", etc. Also note सवारी "ride" – from adj. सवार "mounted" – which has acquired the extended meaning "passenger":

   डिब्बे में चार सवारियाँ थीं.
   There were four passengers in the compartment (male or female).

§ 49. There is a large number of masculine nouns ending in -ई. They often coincide with natural gender:

1. *tadbhav* nouns: धोबी "washerman", मोची "cobbler", माली "gardener", also मोती "pearl", घी "ghee", दही "curd", हाथी "elephant".
2. *tatsam* nouns in -ई represent masc. nom. of Skt. derivatives in -इन् meaning "having X" or "engaged in X": योगी "yogi", अधिकारी

"official, person in authority", विपक्षी "opponent, adversary", मंत्री "minister".

3. *videśī* masculine nouns in -ई are all of Persian or Arabic origin. They usually coincide with natural gender: आदमी "man", दर्ज़ी "tailor", हलवाई "sweetmeat seller", तबलची "tabla-player" (-ची is possibly a Turkish suffix), मुंशी "scribe".

All these follow the 3rd declension (§ 37).

§ 50. Nouns ending in -उ and -ऊ are masculine or feminine, *tadbhav* or *tatsam*, rarely *videśī*. Gender has to be learnt for each individual noun. The masculine follow the 3rd declension (§ 37), the feminine the 4th (§ 39).

§ 51. Nouns ending in a consonant (or, technically, an inherent -अ which is not pronounced) form the 3rd and 4th declinations (§§ 36 and 39). Apart from natural gender in words like पुरुष masc. "man", ठाकुर masc. "landlord", किसान masc. "peasant", औरत fem. "woman", बहिन fem. "sister", gender has to be learnt for each individual noun. However, the following rules may be deduced.

§ 52. Masculine are

1. nouns ending in -पन and -आव: बचपन "childhood", भोलापन "simpleness", घेराव "gherao, encirclement".
2. abstract *tatsam* in -त्व and -य: पितृत्व "paternity", राज्य "kingdom".
3. *neo-tatsam* agent nouns in -अक and -कार: लेखक "author", अध्यापक "teacher", साहित्यकार "litterateur", संगीतकार "composer".

§ 53. Femine are:

1. most verb stems used as nouns: मार "beating", लूट "looting", बाढ़ "flood".
2. masc. nouns in -ई denoting profession or occupation form their feminine in -इन: धोबिन "washerwoman or washerman's wife", मालिन "gardener's wife", नाइन "barber's wife", ठकुराइन "thākur's wife"; but note दुलहन "bride" from दूल्हा "bridegroom".

3. Nouns ending in -आहट or -आवट are feminine: घबराहट "confusion", बनावट "fabrication, sham".
4. *videśī* abstract nouns of Arabic or Persian origin ending in -अत and -इश are feminine: ज़रूरत "necessity", सिफ़ारिश "recommendation".

§ 54. Nouns with variable gender.

1. Masculine nouns denoting male human beings may be changed into feminine nouns by GN-marked modifiers when they refer to females: मेरा दोस्त "my friend" masc., मेरी दोस्त "my friend" fem., हमारा मेहमान "our guest", हमारी मेहमान "our guest" fem., बड़े नेता "great leader" masc. (honorific pl.), बड़ी नेता "great leader" fem.
Also: मेरी बेटी तुम्हारी नौकर थोड़े ही है.

My daughter is hardly your servant.

There is a specific fem. form नौकरानी which is used when a concrete, specific female person is referred to.

If a GN-marked modifier is absent, the verb will usually indicate the gender.

2. Some *videśī* nouns may vary in gender from one speaker to another: रूमाल "handkerchief" (masc. or fem.), टिकट "ticket" (masc. or fem.).

§ 55. The nouns ओर and तरफ़ "direction" are normally feminine, but may occur as masc. in certain contexts:

मैदान की ओर (तरफ़)	in the direction of the field
मैदान के दोनों ओर (तरफ़)	on both sides of the field
मैदान के (की) एक ओर (तरफ़)	on one side of the field
मैदान के (की) उस ओर (तरफ़)	on the other side of the field

§ 56. General terms such as व्यक्ति "person", बच्चा "child", नौकर "servant" (cf. § 54.1 above), etc. are normally masculine, but may refer to females without changing gender or form:

उस व्यक्ति ने मेरी मदद की.	That person (man or woman) helped me.
मिस लतिका बच्चा थोड़े ही है.	Miss Latikā is hardly a child.

NUMBER.

§ 57. Hindī has two numbers: singular and plural. The number is unmistakably indicated in the 1st, 2nd and 4th declensions, but in the 3rd declension (§ 36) sing. and pl. coincide in the direct case. Ambiguity is usually avoided (a) by GN-marked adjectives modifying such nouns, (b) by verbal endings, or (c) simply by the context. Note here the pronouns of address तुम and आप which are always formally pl. regardless of whether one or several persons are meant (see §§ 131, 135, 137).

§ 58. The plural is commonly used for the singular to express respect:

गान्धी जी कहते थे.	Gāndhī used to say.
पिता जी बाग में खड़े हैं.	Father is standing in the garden.

For the honorific particle जी see § 434.

§ 59. A periphrastic plural, formed by adding the word लोग "people" to the noun (or pronoun, cf. § 139), may occur, especially in the spoken language. It generally marks the plural as a class:

अफ़सर लोग देखते थे, मगर कुछ कह नहीं सकते.

The officers used to notice [it], but they could not say anything.

क्या पादरी लोग सफ़ेद चोगे के नीचे कुछ नहीं पहनते.

Don't the priests wear anything under [their] white gown[s]?

§ 60. If the periphrastic plural is in oblique case, only लोग is inflected:

अफ़सर लोगों ने सब देखा.	The officers saw everything.

§ 61. After cardinals or after words signifying multitude (कुछ, कई, इतने, उतने, जितने, कितने, बहुत, etc.) either singular or plural of what is being measured may occur:

दो प्याला चाय	two cups of tea
कितने प्याले चाय	how many cups of tea?
तीन सेर दूध	three seers of milk
तीन महीने के बाद	after three months
चार महीनों में	in four months

उस ने हज़ार रुपया रमेश से लिया है. — He has borrowed a thousand rupees from Rameś.

दो सौ रुपये दे दीजिए. — Please give two hundred rupees.

कई रात से दंगा हो रहा है. — The riot has been going on for several nights.

बहुत दिन के बाद मदन वापस आया. — After many days Madan returned.

दो दिनों में मेला ख़त्म हो जाएगा. — The fair will end in two days.

§ 62. Certain nouns in Hindī differ in meaning depending on the number:

1. छुट्टी fem. means "leave" in sing. and "holidays" in pl.:

मुझे दो महीने की छुट्टी चाहिये. — I need two months leave.

छुट्टियों में हम शिमला जाते हैं. — We [usually] go to Śimlā during the holidays.

2. सीढ़ी fem. means "step [of a staircase]" in sing. and "staircase" in pl.:

वह एक ही सीढ़ी नीचे उतरी. — She descended only one step.

तारा ने सीढ़ियों पर मोमबत्ती रख दी. — Tārā put the candle on the staircase.

3. कपड़ा sing. means cloth, कपड़े pl. means clothes:

कितना कपड़ा चाहिये? — How much cloth do you need?

ये कपड़े धोबी को दे दीजिए! — Give these clothes to the washerman.

4. गर्मी fem. and सर्दी fem. mean "heat" and "cold" in singular, but refer to the hot and cold seasons in plural:

बहुत गर्मी लग रही है. — It is very hot.

गर्मियों में हम शिमला जाते हैं. — We go to Śimlā in the hot season.

§ 63. Note the idiomatic expressions भूखों, प्यासों, जाड़ों मरना "die of hunger/thirst/cold". The obl. pl. of the noun is always **without** postposition:

बेचारा जाड़ों मर गया. — The poor fellow died of cold.

§ 64. *videśī* plural formations have entered the Hindī language and are treated in different ways:

1. The English plural "fees" is rendered as फ़ीस fem. **sing.** with a regular plural फ़ीसें.

2. The Arabic singular ख़बर means "news" in Hindī and is treated as a fem. sing.. The corresponding Arabic plural अख़बार is masc. sing. in Hindī and means "newspaper".
3. The Persian-Arabic plural ending -आत remains plural in Hindī: कागज़ात masc.pl. "papers, documents", कागज़ sing. means "paper", जवाहरात, जवाहिरात masc.pl. "jewels, jewellery", जवाहर, जवाहिर sing. "jewel", हालात masc.pl. "conditions, circumstances".
4. The Persian plural-ending -आन may be both sing. and pl. in Hindī: बाग़ान masc. sg. "plantation", masc. pl. "gardens" (from बाग़ "garden").

CASE.

§ 65. There are three cases in Hindī: direct, oblique and vocative. In the singular, the direct and oblique cases of nouns of the 2nd, 3rd and 4th declensions are identical (see §§ 34, 36, 39), but the context makes it clear whether the intended case is direct or oblique.

THE DIRECT CASE.

§ 66. The direct case is used for (1) the grammatical subject in the subjective construction (see § 323), (2) for the direct object when it does not take the postposition को (see § 81.1), and (3) for adverbial clauses of time and space:

लड़का कुत्ता देख रहा है.	A boy is looking at a dog.
वे पढ़ी-लिखी लड़की नहीं चाहते.	They do not want an educated girl.
कुछ रास्ता राम और मोहन साथ-साथ चलते रहे.	Rām and Mohan continued to walk some distance together.
सारा दिन बिना खाए पिए वह चलता रहा.	He kept walking all day without food or drink.
रामू की बहू दो महीना हुआ प्रथम बार ससुराल आई थी.	Two months ago Rāmū's young wife had come for the first time to [her] in-laws' house.

THE OBLIQUE CASE.

§ 67. The oblique case is obligatory before all postpositions:

वह कमरे से निकला.	He came out of the room.
किताब मेज़ पर पड़ी है.	The book is lying on the table.
लड़कियों से बातचीत करता रहा.	He kept talking to the girls.
डिब्बे में दो ग्रादमी बैठे थे.	Two men were sitting in the compartment.

§ 68. The postposition can be omitted, but the oblique case remains. This happens in the different types of adverbial clauses:

1. adverbs of time, especially if the adverbial clause consists of two or more words:

उन दिनों हम इलाहाबाद में रहते थे.	In those days we lived in Allahabad.
ग्रगले साल मैं चला जाऊँगा.	I'll go away next year.
किसी दिन मैं उस देश को जाऊँगा.	Some day I'll go to that country.
रोज़ सुबह नौकर चाय लाता है.	The servant brings tea every morning.
इस वक़्त/समय सब लोग सोते थे.	At this time everybody is asleep.

2. adverbs of place:

हमें सीट ऐसी जगह मिली... .	We got a seat in such a place...
उस के सिर बड़ा पाप है.	She has sinned greatly. (Lit. There is a great sin on her head.)
सिलाई तो इसी के ज़िम्मे रहती थी.	The stitching remained in her charge.

3. adverbs of direction:

वह ग्रागरे जा रहा है.	He is going to Āgrā.
मैं ग्रपने घर जा रही हूँ.	I am going home.
इस पार से उस पार तैर रहा था.	He was swimming from this shore to the other [shore].

4. in a multitude of adverbial clauses where the postposition can be easily supplied, but its omission does not obscure the meaning:

पीठ के बल तैरना	to swim on the back
किसी न किसी तरह	in one way or another
इस के सम्बन्ध	in connection with this
उस के जिस्म के सहारे	with the support of his/her body
चाय लाने के बहाने	under the pretext of bringing tea

भूखों मरना	to die of hunger (cf. § 63)
रोशनदान के रास्ते आ गया होगा.	It must have come through the ventilator..

5. Oblique infinitive without postposition is used with verbs of motion to express the finality or intention of the action(s) (see § 394.1):

मोहन दूध लाने गया है.	Mohan has gone to fetch milk.
घूमने आ रहे हो?	Are you coming for a walk?
वह टिकट खरीदने गई.	She went to buy tickets.

The deleted postposition in these cases is के लिए.

VOCATIVE.

§ 69. The vocative case is used for addressing or calling somebody. In the **sing.**, only masc. nouns of the 1st masc. declension have a special vocative form ending in -ए, as for example बेटे "son!", in all other declensions the vocative sing. is identical to the direct case (except in certain *tatsam* words where the Skt. voc. may occur (see § 38.1). This may happen in the 1st masc. declension also: बेटा "son!"
Vocative **plural** is formed by omitting the nasalization of the final -ओं in the oblique plural: आदमियो "men!" बहिनो और भाइयो "sisters and brothers!".

ARTICLES.

§ 70. There are no specific definite and indefinite articles in Hindī. लड़का may mean "a boy" or "the boy" according to context:

लड़का आ रहा है.	A boy is coming. The boy is coming.
लड़की कुत्ता देख रही है.	A girl is looking at a dog. The girl is looking at the dog.
आदमी आ गये.	Men arrived. The men arrived.

§ 71. The direct object may be particularized by the postposition को:

लड़की कुत्ते को देख रही है. The girl is looking at the dog.

See § 81.1.

§ 72. To mark definiteness, demonstrative pronouns may modify the noun:

वे आदमी आ गये. Those/the men arrived.

§ 73. If indefiniteness is to be indicated, Hindī resorts to the indefinite pronoun कोई in lieu of an indefinite article:

किसी गाँव में रहता होगा. He must be living in a/some village.

ज़रूर कोई जानवर कुएँ में गिर कर मर गया होगा.
Surely an animal/some animal must have fallen into the well and died.

§ 74. The numeral एक "one" is often translated into English as an indefinite article. This is, however, not the meaning in Hindī: एक is usually a **definite** article, **one particular** X.

उस रात एक अबदुल को नींद नहीं आई.
That night [one particular] Abdul could not sleep.

उधर एक होटल है. There is a hotel over there.

बोट क्लब पर एक किसान के मरने से तनाव
Tension at the Boat Club on account of the death of a peasant

Although the correct English translation is often the indefinite article "a", in Hindī एक refers to a particular hotel resp. peasant.

§ 75. Compare the following sentences:

पादरी स्ताफ़ रूम में पहुँच गया. वहाँ पाल एक कोने में खड़ा कोई मैगज़ीन देख रहा था.

The priest reached the staff room. There Pāl was standing in a corner looking at a magazine.

It is obvious that Pāl can stand only in one particular corner of the room, but he is looking at some magazine out of an indefinite number of magazines.

वोटों की गिनती के ताजा संकेत बताते हैं कि किसी एक दल को साफ़ बहुमत शायद ही मिले.

The fresh signs of the vote-counting indicate that a single party may get a clear majority.

> कोई fills the funtion of an indefinite article here, and एक serves the purpose of stating that it is going to be a particular party although it is as yet not known which one.

POSTPOSITIONS.

§ **76.** Postpositions are grammatical function markers, placed **after** the syntactic unit they govern. Postpositions govern nouns, pronouns, numerals, adverbs, substantival adjectives and verbal forms such as the infinitive and participles, all of these in the **oblique case**:

कमरे में	in the room	मुझ को	me, to me
गरीबों से	from the poor	लिखने से	by/through writing

§ 77. Since postpositions mark the end of a syntactic unit they may be followed by a short pause in speech (see § 459).

§ 78. Postpositions are of two kinds:

1. simple pp. i.e. ने, को, पर, में, से, तक
2. compound pp. such as के लिए, के पास, के नीचे, के पीछे, के साथ, के ऊपर, etc.

§ **79.** Simple postpositions, which correspond to the old Indo-Aryan case-endings, often have several different meanings and functions, just as the old cases had. The choice of postposition is often idiomatic. Simple postpositions can be written together with its main word: कमरेमें, मेज़पर.

SIMPLE POSTPOSITIONS.

§ **80.** The postposition ने has one exclusive function: it indicates the subject in sentences where the finite, object-taking verb is in a tense using the perfective aspect (see § 324) .

उस ने किताब पढ़ी.	He/she read the book.
राम ने चाय पी ली.	Rām drank tea.
मैं ने कहा.	I said.

§ **81.** The postposition को has several functions:

1. it marks *the direct object*, i.e. the accusative, if the direct object is particularized (cf. § 71):

मैं सीता को देख रही है.	I am looking at Sītā.

दर्ज़ी को बुलाम्रो!	Call the tailor!
इसी किताब को पढ़िये!	Read this book!

2. it marks *the direct object* in sentences with double accusative, i.e. objective completion:

प्रजा ने राम को राजा बनाया.	The people made Rām king.
मैं तुम को अपना भाई समझता हूँ.	I consider you my brother.
वह निर्धनता को पाप मानता है.	He considers poverty a sin.

3. it marks *the indirect object* , i.e. the dative:

मैं रोज़ मोहन को फल देती हूँ.	I give fruit to Mohan every day.
माँ बच्चों को कहानियाँ सुनाती है.	The mother tells stories to the children.

4. it marks the logical subject in constructions with infinitive + होना, पड़ना and चाहिये (cf. §§ 403-405) – note that *the logical subject* **syntactically** is in the dative, i.e. it is *the indirect object* (cf. § 473):

मुझ को जाना है.	I have to go.
सीता को पेन्सिल चाहिये.	Sītā needs a pencil.
उस को काम करना पड़ता है.	He/she has to work.

5. it marks the logical subject in sentences expressing perceptions and feelings of all kinds. Again the syntagm marked by को is grammatically *the indirect object* (cf. § 472):

मुझ को बड़ी ख़ुशी है.	I am very happy. (lit. Great happiness is to me.)
उस को लज्जा आई.	He/she felt ashamed.
क्या आप को सर्दी लगी?	Did you get cold?
उस को दुख हुआ.	He became sad.
लड़की को बुख़ार है.	The girl has a fever.
मुझ को भूख लगती है.	I am hungry.

6. it is used to mark adverbs of time and place :

वह शाम को आया.	He came in the evening.
इतवार को आइये!	Please come on Sunday!
वह अपने देश को लौट गया.	He returned to his homeland.
मैं बाज़ार को जा रहा हूँ.	I am going to the market.

§ 82. However, with adverbs of time and place को can be deleted but the oblique case remains (§ 68.1-3):

मैं कलकत्ते जा रहा हूँ. — I am going to Calcutta.
उस रात चार डाकू आए. — That night four dacoits came.

§ 83. Like को, the postposition से has several functions:

1. it indicates *the agent* in passive and causative sentences (see § 372 and § 366) resp.):

राम से शत्रु मारा गया. — The enemy was killed by Rām.
बकरा शेर से खाया गया है. — The goat has been eaten by the lion.
मोहन से चिट्ठी नहीं लिखी जाती. — Mohan cannot write the letter.
लड़के से दौड़ा नहीं गया. — The boy could not run.
यह काम नौकर से करवा दो! — Get this work done by the servant!
माँ नानी से बच्चों को कहानियाँ सुनवाती है. — The mother makes the grandmother tell stories to the children.

2. it indicates *the indirect object* with verbs such as कहना, पूछना, मिलना, डरना, लड़ना, etc.:

पिता ने गाँववालों से बातचीत की. — Father talked to the villagers.
राजा ने नगरपाल से पूछा - आप उस आदमी से कहाँ मिले? — The king asked the Mayor: where did you meet that man?
मोहन ने सीता से कहा कि मैं तुम से प्यार करता हूँ. — Mohan said to Sītā that he loved her.
कुत्ता बिल्ली से डर रहा है. — The dog is afraid of the cat.
कुत्ता बिल्ली से लड़ रहा है. — The dog is fighting with the cat.
बन्दर बच्चे से खाना चुरा रहा है. — The monkey is stealing food from the child.

3. it is used in comparisons to mark the object with which something or somebody is compared (see §§ 214, 219) :

मोहन राम से बड़ा है. — Mohan is bigger than Rām.
मेरी गाड़ी तुम्हारी गाड़ी से बड़ी है. — My car is bigger than yours.
वह सब से बड़े मकान में रहता है. — He lives in the biggest house.

4. it is used in adverbial functions with the basic meaning "from" (ablative) or "with" (instrumental):

लड़की कुएँ से पानी लाती है. The girl brings water from the well.
वह कलकत्ते से लौट आया. He returned from Calcutta.
वह हैज़े से मर गया. He died of cholera.
दही दूध से बनता है. Yoghurt is made from milk.
औरत रस्से से गाय को बाँध रही है. The woman is tying up the cow with a rope.
फल चाकू से काटो! Cut the fruit with a knife!
किसान हल से खेत जोटता है. The peasant plows the field with a plough.
मैं बीस साल से यहाँ रहता हूँ. I have lived here for twenty years.
वह दस घंटों से सो रहा है. He has been sleeping for ten hours.

5. Regarding the oblique infinitive + से see § 397.

§ 84. The postposition पर has the basic locative meaning "on. at". It is used:

1. in adverbial phrases to denote an adverbs of place or time:
मीरा छत पर खड़ी है. Mīrā is standing on the roof.
पेड़ पर फल है. There is fruit on the tree.
वह दरवाज़े पर बैठा है. He is sitting at the door.
वह वक्त पर आया. He came on time.
मैं ठीक समय पर पहुँचा. I arrived right on time.

2. in idiomatic usages with certain compound verbs, i.e. noun + verb:
जीवों पर दया करो! Be kind to living beings!
ईश्वर पर विश्ववास करो! Believe in God!
उन्हों ने मुसलमानों पर हमला किया. They attacked the Muslims.
वह नौकरों पर क्रोध करता है. He [often] gets angry with the servants.
अमृतलाल रोज़ सीता पर विचार करता है. Amṛtlāl thinks of Sītā every day.

3. Regarding the oblique infinitive + पर see § 395.

§ 85. The postposition में has the basic locative meaning "in, within". It is used

1. in adverbial phrases denoting place, time and manner:
माँ घर में खाना पका रही है. Mother is cooking in the house.

मैं शहर में रहता हूँ. — I live in the city.
चाय में चीनी नहीं है. — There is no sugar in the tea.
मकान एक साल में तैयार हुआ. — The house became ready in one year.
गरमियों में मैं पहाड़ पर जाता हूँ. — I go to the hills in the hot season.
राजा ने गुप्त में चालीस आदमियों को भेजा. — The king secretly sent forty men.
वे सब बंगाली में बोल रहे थे. — They were all talking in Bengali.

2. to express the English "have" in sentences where actual "possession" is doubtful or impossible. For example:

घर में चार खिड़कियाँ हैं. — The house has four windows.
नेता में हिम्मत नहीं. — The leader has no courage.

3. in idiomatic expressions:

छाया पण्डित के बच्चों में बड़ी दिलचस्पी लेती है. — Chāyā takes great interest in the pandit's children.
यह किताब मुझे दो रुपये में मिली. — I got this book for two rupees.
घोड़ा कितने में बेचेंगे? — How much are you selling the horse for?

4. in the superlative if the object of comparison is expressed (see § 214):

इन लड़कों में राम सब से अच्छा है. — Among these boys Rām is [the] best.

§ 86. The postposition तक means "up to, until" and is used in adverbial phrases denoting time and place:

वह कल तक शहर में रहेगा. — He will stay in town until tomorrow.
हम शहर की सीमा तक साथ साथ गए. — We went together up to the town limit.

§ 87. The combination of से-तक is used to indicate distance in time and place:

सुबह से शाम तक वह काम करता रहता है. — He keeps working from morning to night.
यहाँ से गाँव तक चार मील हैं. — There are four miles from here to the village.
रेलगाड़ी इलाहाबाद से लखनऊ तक नहीं रुकती. — From Allahabad to Lucknow the train does not stop.

§ 88. Sometimes two simple postpositions can be joined for the purpose of clarity:

लड़का घर में से निकला.	The boy came out from the house (lit. "from in(side) the house").
वह किताब मेज़ पर से ले रहा है.	He is taking the book from the table (lit. "from on the table").

COMPOUND POSTPOSITIONS.

§ 89. Compound postpositions usually contain the genitive-marker in oblique sing. + a noun, a substantival adjective or an adverb in the oblique case. Historically, these postpositions developed out of a larger unit ending in one of the simple postpositions, for example **X के कारण** "because of X" originally read **X के कारण से** "from the reason of X", **X के सामने** "in front of, opposite X" from **X के सामने पर** "at the front of X", **X की तरफ़** "towards X" from **X की तरफ़ में** "in the direction of X". As a result of this way of creating compound postpositions the number is not fixed and may continue to increase, whereas the number of simple postpositions is fixed.

§ 90. One single compound postposition has retained the final simple postposition: **के बारे में** "concerning, regarding, about":

हम युद्ध के बारे में बोल रहे थे.	We were talking about the war.

§ 91. Since the possessive forms of the 1st and 2nd personal pronouns are in themselves genitive, the genitive-marker **के/की** is eliminated:

मेरे साथ "together with me", **हमारी ओर** "towards us", **तुम्हारे सामने** "in front of you", but **उस के साथ** "with him/her", **आप की ओर** "towards you", **किस के सामने** "in front of whom?".

§ 92. Some compound postpositions have **से** alternating with **के**:

के पहले / से पहले	"earlier, before"
के पूर्व / से पूर्व	"earlier, before"
के बाहर / से बाहर	"outside"
के आगे / से आगे	"before, in front of"

§ 93. Most compound postpositions are used to mark **adverbial clauses:**

लड़के पेड़ के नीचे बातचीत कर रहे हैं. The boys are talking under the tree.

मेरे सामने मेज़ रख दो. Put the table in front of me.

पुल के ऊपर जाइये! Go over the bridge!

वह मोहन के साथ आया. He came with Mohan.

तुम पण्डित की तरह बोल रहे हो. You are speaking like a pandit.

एक हफ़्ते के बाद वह वापस आ गया. He returned after one week.

§ 94. The compound postpositions के द्वारा (or simply द्वारा) and के ज़रिये are used as alternatives to से to indicate the agent in causative and passive clauses (cf. §§ 366, 372) :

प्रधानमन्त्री के द्वारा निश्चित किया गया है कि... It has been decided by the Prime Minister that ...

§ 95. In the comparative and the superlative the simple से which marks the object of comparison can be replaced with the more elaborate compound postpositions की अपेक्षा, की तुलना etc., all of course literally meaning "in comparison with" (see § 215).

§ 96. The compound postposition के पास has three usages:

1. as an adverb of place "in the vicinity of, near":

गाँव के पास कुआँ है. There is a well near the village.

मेरे पास आओ! Come to me!

2. together with होना it indicates possession:

सीता के पास लाल गाड़ी है. Sītā has a red car.

इस शहर में मेरे पास दो मकान हैं. I have two houses in this city.

3. it may indicate the indirect object :

पिताजी के मर जाने की सूचना तार द्वारा उन के पास आई. The notice of [his] father's death came to him via a telegram.

मेरे पास आओ! Come to me!

§ 97. The compound postpositions के बिना, के मारे, के सिवा/सिवाय can be inverted for emphasis:

बिना पैसे के "without money", मारे भूख के "on account of hunger", सिवा राम के "except Rām".

§ 98. बिना + oblique perfective participle does not carry the element के. बिना can be placed before or after the participle (see § 385):

पढ़े बिना उस ने परीक्षा पास की.	He passed the exam without studying.
बिना मुझे देखे वह चाय पीता रहा.	He kept on drinking tea without having looked at me.
बिना किसी से कुछ कहे हुए वह चला गया.	He went away without having said anything to anybody.

THE GENITIVE-MARKER का, की, के.

§ 99. The gender-number-marked genitive-marker का is often classified as a postposition. However, it **never** marks the end of a syntactic unit which is the characteristic of postpositions. The genitive-marker is inflected like an adjective:

	Sing.	Plur.
Masc. Dir.	का	के
Masc. Obl.	के	के
Fem. Dir.	की	की
Fem. Obl.	की	की

§ 100. The genitive-marker takes its gender and number from the noun, substantival adjective, adverb or verbal form **that follows**. It is preceded by a noun, pronoun etc. always in the oblique case:

मोहन का बेटा	Mohan's son
उस का घर	his/her house
बच्चों के खिलौने	the children's toys
पाँच वर्ष का लड़का	a five-year old boy
सोने का कमरा	a bedroom

पीने का पानी	drinking water
एक रुपये की चीनी	suger for one rupee
लाहौर की सड़क	the road to Lahore
कल्कत्ते का व्यापारी	a merchant from Calcutta
वहाँ का मन्दिर	the temple there
नीचे का चारपाई	the lower bed/the bed downstairs
नीम का पेड़	a neem tree
मिट्टी का बरतन	a clay utensil

§ 101. If the modified word is in the oblique case, the genitive marker is also in the oblique case.

आम के पेड़ से फल गिरे.	Fruit fell from the mango tree.
पाँच वर्ष के लड़के ने कहा.	The five-year old boy said.
वहाँ के मन्दिरों में वहुत वन्दर होते हैं.	There are many monkeys in the temples there.
गाँव के बूढ़े किसानों ने हमें यह दिखा दिया.	The village's old peasants showed us this.
किताब खाने की मेज़ पर रख दो!	Put the book on the dining table!
राम की बेटियों से बातचीत कीजिए!	Please talk to Rām's daughters!

PRONOUNS.

§ 102. Hindī has the following types of pronouns: demonstrative, personal, possessive, possessive-reflexive, reflexive, reciprocal, interrogative, indefinite, and relative.

§ 103. Pronouns are either independent or adjectival. They occur both in singular and plural. They are not gender-marked with the exception of possessive and possessive-reflexive pronouns functioning as adjectives.

§ 104. Pronouns have direct or oblique case. The oblique case can be divided in three groups:

1) oblique before the postposition ने
2) oblique before all other postpositions
3) special object form (direct or indirect object), semantically equivalent to oblique form + the postposition को

§ 105. Possessive pronouns are usually formed by adding a genitive marker (का, की, के) to the oblique case of the relevant pronoun: किस का "whose", किसी का "somebody's", उस का "his/her".
See §§ 99-101.

§ 106. Personal possessive pronouns have special GN-marked forms: मेरा, तेरा, हमारा, तुम्हारा. आप is an exception: आप का, की, के.
See §§ 142, 143.

§ 107. The use of direct and oblique case follows the same rules as those for nouns. See §§ 65-67.

DEMONSTRATIVE PRONOUNS.

§ 108. There are two demonstrative pronouns: वह "that" and यह "this". They exist in singular and plural.

§ **109.** Tables.

	Sing.		Plur.	
Direct case	यह	वह	ये	वे
Oblique + ने	इस	उस	इन्हों	उन्हों
Oblique + pp.	इस	उस	इन	उन
Special obj. form	इसे	उसे	इन्हें	उन्हें
Poss. form	इस का	उस का	इन का	उन का

§ **110.** यह "this", वह "that", ये "these", वे "those" are demonstrative pronouns, but they also function as 3rd person personal pronouns. They are **not** in themselves gender-marked (gender is usually marked in the verbal ending). As **demonstrative** pronouns they normally occur as modifiers to nouns, as **personal** pronouns they function independently:

यह कागज़ काला है, वह कागज़ लाल है.	This paper is black, that paper is red.
वह लड़की राम की बेटी है.	That girl is Rām's daughter.
वह बहुत सुन्दर है.	She is very beautiful.
ये आदमी दिल्ली में रहते हैं.	These men live in Delhi.
वे कल आए.	They came yesterday.

§ **111.** The oblique forms इस, उस, इन, उन, whether independent or as modifiers, are always followed by a postposition:

मैं इस लड़की से बात कर रहा हूँ.	I am talking to this girl.
उस ने कहा.	He/she said.
यह किताब उस मेज़ पर रख दो!	Put this book on that table!
वह इस बिल्ली को खिलाती है.	She [usually] feeds this cat.
वह उस को खाना खिलाती है.	She feeds him/her.
बच्चे उन बड़े पेड़ों के नीचे बैठे हैं.	The children are sitting under those big trees.

§ **112.** When the pronoun modifies a noun, the postposition can be deleted in certain adverbial expressions. See § 68. 1-5 and § 230.

उस दिन तुम क्यों नहीं आए?	Why didn't you come that day?
उस समय मैं बम्बई रहती थी.	At that time I lived in Bombay.

§ 113. Before the postposition ने, ये/वे have the oblique form इन्हों/उन्हों:

उन्हों ने मोहन को देखा. They saw Mohan.
इन्हों ने मुझ से पूछा. They asked me.

§ 114. The special object forms इसे/उसे, इन्हें/उन्हें are semantically equivalent to इस/उस को, इन/उन को. If there are two objects in the same sentence requiring को, one takes को and the other the special object form to avoid repetition of को:

मैं ने उसे देखा. I saw him/her.
इसे ले लो! Take this one!
उसे इस पुस्तक को दे देना! Give him/her this book!
उसे मोहन को दीजिए! Give it to Mohan!

§ 115. Plural ये/वे are used for sing. to mark respect:

रास्ते पर मैं ने अपने पिता जी को देखा. वे कोई पड़ोसियों से बातचीत कर रहे थे.

I saw my father on the street. He was talking to some neighbours.

§ 116. For possessive forms see possessive pronouns § 142.

EMPHATIC FORMS OF DEMONSTRATIVE PRONOUNS.

§ 117. The emphatic, enclitic particle ही (see § 440) is in certain forms contracted with the pronoun, and in others it follows immediately after:

	Sing.		Plur.	
Direct case	यही	वही	ये ही	वे ही
Oblique case	इसी	उसी	इन्हीं	उन्हीं
Object form	इसे ही	उसे ही	इन्हें ही	उन्हें ही
Poss. form	इसी का	उसी का	इन्हीं का	उन्हीं का

इसी साड़ी को ले लीजिए! Take this saree!
वही आदमी आगरे से है. That man is from Āgrā.

The English would stress the demonstrative pronouns in the above examples.

§ 118. Note the nasalisation of the particle in the oblique plural:

उन्हीं दिनों में ...	During those very days ...

IDIOMATIC USE OF यह/वह, ये/वे.

§ 119. यह/वह, ये/वे sometimes have an adverbial meaning "here, now" and "there, so, so much":

यह आया!	Here he comes!
अँगूठियाँ ये रखी हैं.	The rings are here.
अँगूठी वह रही, मैं यहाँ खड़ा हूँ.	The ring is there. I'm standing here.

§ 120. यह/वह along with देखो/देखिए, लो/लीजिए are used as deictic interjections:

वह देखो, मोहन आ गया है.	Look, Mohan has come!
यह लो, वह आया!	Look, here he comes!
यह लीजिए, गाड़ी खड़ी हो गई!	Look, the train has stopped!

PERSONAL PRONOUNS.

§ 121. Proper personal pronouns exist only in 1st and 2nd person singular and plural and the honorific pronoun आप which is 3rd pers. plural. As 3rd person personal pronouns demonstrative pronouns are used. See § 110.

§ 122. Table – First person:

	Sing.	Plur.
Direct case	मैं	हम
Oblique + ने	मैं ने	हम ने
Oblique + pp.	मुझ	हम
Special obj. form	मुझे	हमें
Poss. form	मेरा	हमारा

§ 123. 1st person sing. मैं "I" and 1st person plur. हम "we" are not in themselves gender-marked. The gender is indicated in the verb-ending. मैं and हम are used as in English:

मैं यहाँ रहता हूँ.	I (masc.) live here.
मैं उन से पूछूँगी.	I (fem.) will ask them.
हम दिल्ली से आए हैं.	We (masc.) have come from Delhi.
हम हिन्दी बोलती हैं.	We (fem.) speak Hindī.

§ 124. हम is sometimes used for मैं, especially in Eastern Hindī:

क्या हम जाएँ?	May I go?
हम ने किया.	I did.
मोहन ने हमें यह किताब दी.	Mohan gave me this book.

§ 125. The periphrastic plural हम लोग is often used in the spoken language:

हम लोग पटना जा रहे हैं.	We (masc.) are going to Paṭnā.
हम लोग खाना पका रही हैं.	We (fem.) are preparing food.

§ 126. The oblique case before ने is मैं ने and हम ने resp.:

मैं ने उत्तर दिया कि हम ने स्टेशन पर सामान छोड़ दिया था.
I answered that we had left our luggage at the station.

मैं ने खाना पकाया और शाम को हम ने खा लिया.
I prepared the food and in the evening we ate it.

हम ने लड़के को फल दिया.	We gave the boy fruit.

§ 127. However, if there is an attribute to मैं before ने the oblique form is मुझ:

मुझ अभागी ने कुछ नहीं देखा.	I, unfortunate one, saw nothing.

Other oblique forms:

सीता मुझ से मिली.	Sītā met me.
नौकर ने हम से पूछ लिया.	The servant asked us.
मुझे/मुझ को मोमबत्ती दो!	Give me a candle!
वे हमें/हम को देख रहे थे.	They were looking at us.

§ 128. Possessive forms, see Possessive pronouns §§ 142-144.

PRONOUNS OF ADDRESS: तू, तुम, and आप.

§ 129. Table – Second person:

	Sing.	Plur.
Direct case	तू	तुम
Oblique + ने	तू ने	तुम ने
Oblique + pp.	तुझ	तुम
Special obj. form	तुझे	तुम्हें
Poss. form	तेरा	तुम्हारा

§ 130. The honorific pronoun आप takes the form आप in all cases and forms. It is not in itself gender-marked. Cf. § 123.

§ 131. Formally, तू is 2nd pers. sing., तुम 2nd pers. plur., and आप 3rd pers. plur. They are not in themselves gender-marked. Cf. § 123.

तू बोलता/बोलती है.	You speak.
तुम बोलते/बोलती हो.	You speak.
आप बोलते/बोलती हैं.	You speak.

USE OF तू.

§ 132. तू is used in two distinct ways:

A. in intimate and affectionate speech between, for example, mother and child, between lovers in private, in prayers and in poetry;
B. to express contempt, disgust or anger, often in speaking to somebody considered socially inferior:

बेटे, तू क्या कर रहा है?	What are you doing, son?
क्या तू शीला के घर जाएगा?	Will you go to Śīlā's place?
हे भगवान, तू ही मुझे बचा सकता है.	O God, only you can save me!
प्रियतम, तू मेरी हाला है!	Beloved, you are my wine!
तू बिलकुल पागल है!	You are completely crazy!
पापी, तू इन्सान की खाल में भेड़िया है.	You sinner, you are a wolf in the guise of a human being!
उल्लू, तू क्या कह रहा है?	What are you saying, you fool?

§ 133. Oblique form before ने is तू. If an attribute is added, the oblique form is तुझ (cf. § 127):

क्या तू ने यह काम किया, बेटे? Did you do this, [my] son?
तुझ पागल ने यह किया. You crazy one did this.
In all other cases the oblique form is तुझ .

§ 134. For the possessive तेरा see Possessive pronouns § 143 .

USE OF तुम.

§ 135. Like तू, तुम also has two distinct shades of meaning:

A. in addressing family-members of the same age or younger, between friends of the same age, and in all informal relationships;

B. in addressing people whom the speaker considers socially lower than himself, such as servants, coolies, ricksha-pullers; also used by city-people talking to peasants. The rural population often uses तुम even in respectful address, because their dialect may not have an equivalent for आप.

सीता, तुम कल आओगी? Sītā, will you come tomorrow?
क्या हमारा नया अध्यापक तुम को अच्छा लगता है? Do you like our new teacher?
तुम ने अपना जीवन क्यों बरबाद किया? Why did you ruin your life?
क्या तुम मेरा गिरफ़्तार करने आए हो? Have you come to arrest me?
रामू, साहब का सामान सोने के कमरे में रखो! Rāmū, put the master's luggage in the bedroom!
क्या तुम ने रात का खाना बनाया? Did you prepare food for tonight?
क्या तुम इस गाँव में रहते हो? Do you live in this village?
Note that तुम is both direct and oblique form.

§ 136. For the possessive तुम्हारा see Possessive pronouns § 143.

USE OF आप.

§ 137. आप is the formal pronoun of address used to strangers, to superiors, to older people, and in all contexts where तुम would be too familiar and casual. Note that Indian society is far more formal than North American society.

क्या आप रवि की बहिन हैं?	Are you Ravi's sister?
यहाँ आप हिन्दी बोल सकते हैं.	You can speak Hindī here.
क्या आप पिछले हफ़्ते बम्बइ गए?	Did you go to Bombay last week?

§ 138. In literary style, when great formality and respect is required, आप can be used as 3rd person. As it is always honorific, it is plural (see § 58):

आप का जन्म कुरुक्षेत्र में हुआ. He was born in Kurukṣetra.

सन १८८३ आप सपरिवार रिटोली ग्राम में आ गए.
In 1883 he came to village of Riṭolī with his family.

तुलसीदास हिन्दी के प्रसिद्ध कवि थे. आप ने रामचरितमानस लिखा.
Tulsīdās was a famous Hindī poet. He wrote the Rāmcaritmānas.

PERIPHRASTIC PLURAL OF तुम and आप.

§ 139. Formally both तुम and आप are plural – 2nd and 3rd pers. plur. resp. – as the verbal morphemes clearly indicate. However, as pronouns of address तुम and आप are used to address one person as well as several. If there is any doubt about the number intended, the plural marker लोग is added (cf. § 59):

कितने दिन आप लोग यहाँ रहेंगे?	How many days will you (pl.) stay here?
तुम लोगों ने यह किया.	You people did this.

§ 140. Words syntactically belonging to तुम or आप are used in the plural, whether one or several persons are intended:

तुम बच्चे ही हो.	You are only a child. You are only children.
तुम अच्छे लड़के हो.	You are a good boy. You are good boys.
आप कैसे हैं.	How are you?

§ 141. The above rule does not apply to feminine gender:

तुम लड़की ही हो.	You are only a girl.
तुम लड़कियाँ ही हो.	You are only girls.

POSSESSIVE PRONOUNS.

§ 142. In Hindī the genitives of other pronouns function as possessive pronouns. They are formed by adding the GN-marked genitive-marker का (see §§ 99-101) to the oblique case: उस का "his/ her, hers", उन का "their, theirs", आप का "your, yours" (honorific), किस का "whose?", किसी का "someone's", etc.

§ 143. Only the 1st and 2nd pers. personal pronouns have special possessive forms: मेरा "my, mine", हमारा "our, ours", तेरा "your, yours", तुम्हारा "your, yours", all inflected like GN-marked adjectives (see § 203).

§ 144. The possessive pronouns are used both in attributive, i.e. as modifiers, and predicative position:

मेरे बच्चे छोटे हैं.	My children are small.
क्या तुम्हारी बहिनें आ रही हैं?	Are your sisters coming?
उन के देश में लड़ाई हो रही है.	There is war in their country.
मेरा लड़का किस के घर में है?	In whose house is my son?
जिस की लाठी उस की भैंस.	Might is right. (Lit. He who has the stick has the buffalo.)
यह किताब मेरी है.	This book is mine.
वह मकान उन का है.	That house is theirs.
यह गाड़ी किसी की होती होगी.	This car must belong to someone.

THE POSSESSIVE-REFLEXIVE PRONOUN अपना.

§ 145. The GN-marked possessive-reflexive pronoun अपना "one's own" is used for all persons, singular and plural. It takes its meaning from the subject in the sentence:

मैं अपना सामान ला रहा हूँ.	I'm bringing my luggage.
तू अपनी बहिन के साथ जाता है.	You [usually] go with your sister.
शाम को वह अपने घर में खाना खाता है.	In the evening he eats at home (lit. in his own house).
हम अपनी किताबें पढ़ रहे थे.	We were reading our books.
तुम उसे अपने कपड़े देते हो.	You [usually] give him your clothes.
उन्हों ने हमें अपना पता दे दिया.	They gave us their address.
अपना पता लिख लीजिए!	Please write down your address!

§ 146. अपना also refers to the logical subject in sentences such as:

मुझे अपना काम करना चाहिये.	I have to do my work.
सब लोगों को अपना कर्त्तव्य करना है.	Everyone has to do his duty.

Note expressions such as:

अपने देश में	In our [own] country ...

§ 147. अपना may be combined with other possessive pronouns for emphasis:

मेरा अपना घर.	My own house.
उस के अपने पिता.	His own father.

§ 148. Note the difference between अपना and other possessive forms:

मैं अपने भाई से बातचीत कर रहा हूँ.	I am talking to my brother.
वह मेरे भाई से बातचीत कर रहा है.	He is talking to my brother.
वह अपने भाई से बातचीत कर रहा है.	He is talking to his [own] brother.
वह उस के भाई से बातचीत कर रहा है.	He is talking to his [i.e. someone else's] brother.

वे अपना सामान लाए. They brought their [own] luggage.
वे उन का सामान लाए. They brought their [i.e. someone else's] luggage.

REFLEXIVE PRONOUNS.

§ 149. There are three reflexive pronouns in Hindī: आप, स्वयं and खुद, all having the meaning "oneself". Like the possessive-reflexive pronoun अपना, आप, स्वयं and खुद refer to the grammatical or logical subject of the sentence. An emphatic ही is often added:

मैं आप (ही) वहाँ चला गया. I myself went there.
मोहन आप (ही) गरीब है. Mohan himself is poor.
उस ने आप (ही) यह पत्र लिखा. He himself wrote this letter.
or: She herself wrote this letter.
नेता में आप (ही) हिम्मत नहीं है. The leader himself has no courage.

§ 150. In all the examples above the *tadbhav* word आप may be replaced by the *tatsam* word स्वयं or the Persian loanword खुद. Note that the pronunciation of स्वयं is *svayam*, i.e. "m" is pronounced without nasalisation of the preceding vowel.

§ 151. The oblique case of the reflexive pronoun आप – not to be confused with the personal pronoun आप – is अपने or अपने आप. The invariable स्वयं and खुद rarely appear in the oblique case. Examples:

सीता ने अपने (आप) को दोष दिया. Sītā blamed herself.
वह अपने (आप) को अभागी आदमी समझता है.
He considers himself an unfortunate man.
मैं अपने लिए यह करूँगा. I shall do this for myself.

§ 152. When used as an adverb अपने आप means "for one's own sake, of one's own initiative":

मैं अपने आप हिन्दी सीखने लगा. I began to learn Hindī on my own.

§ 153. In some expressions the oblique आपे (actually from the derived noun आपा masc. "ego, one's own self") is used:

वह आपे में नहीं है. He is not himself/in his right mind.

वह छोटी-छोटी बातों पर आपे से बाहर हो जाता है. He gets besides himself over very small matters.

RECIPROCAL PRONOUNS.

§ 154. आपस is actually a collective noun meaning "reciprocity, fellowship". When used with the postposition में or the genitive-marker का it acquires the pronominal meaning "each other, one another":

भाइयों के लिए आपस में लड़ना-झगड़ना अच्छा नहीं है. It isn't good for brothers to quarrel and fight between themselves.

§ 155. The derived invariable adjective आपसी "mutual, reciprocal" can be used:

उन के आपसी सम्बन्ध अच्छे थे. They had a good relationship to each other.

§ 156. As a synonym of आपस में the *tatsam* pronoun परस्पर may be used, especially in literary style:

बच्चे परस्पर मिठाई बाँट लेंगे. The children will divide the sweets between themselves.

§ 157. परस्पर may function as an adjective in Hindī:

इन लोगों में परस्पर बैर है. These people are mutual enemies.

INTERROGATIVE PRONOUNS.

§ 158. There are two interrogative pronouns in Hindī: कौन "who? which?" and क्या "what? which?". They are used both independently and as modifiers.

§ 159. TABLE

	Sing.			Plur.
Dir.	कौन		क्या	कौन
Obl. + ने		किस		किन्हों
Obl. + pp		किस		किन
Spec. obj. form	किसे		क्या	किन्हें
Poss.		किस का		किन का

क्या has an archaic oblique form काहे.

§ 160. Independent कौन refers to **animate** beings:

कौन आया?	Who came?
वे कौन हैं?	Who are they?
कौन मेरी मदद कर सकता?	Who would be able to help me?
कुत्ता किस का है?	Whose dog is it?
किस को किताब दे दी?	To whom did you give the book?
तुम किन से पूछोगे?	Whom (pl.) will you ask?
लड़के ने रास्ते पर किन्हें देखा?	Whom (pl.) did the boy see on the road?

§ 161. The oblique plural किन्हों can only occur independently:

किन्हों ने यह किया है?	Who [among you] have done this?

§ 162. As a modifier कौन refers to both animates and inanimates:

कौन आदमी खेत पर काम कर रहा है?	What man is working in the field?
कौन औरतें खाना पकाती हैं?	What women cook the food?
कौन बैलगाड़ी तुम्हारी है?	Which oxcart is yours?
ये कौन किताबें हैं?	What books are these?
मैं किस सड़क से कल्कत्ते जा सकता हूँ?	By which road can I go to Calcutta?
लड़का किन औरतों के लिए पानी ला रहा है?	For which women is the boy fetching water?

§ 163. The GN-marked suffix -सा, -सी, -से (see § 428 ff.) can be added to कौन which then remains invariable in all numbers and cases. कौन-सा is different from कौन in that it refers to one or more persons or things in a choice of several possibilities. The distinction between कौन and कौन-सा is not rigorously observed, especially in the spoken language.

आज कौन-सा दिन है?	What day is it today?
कौन-सी किताबें मेज़ पर हैं?	Which books are on the table?
कौन-से आदमी गाँव रहते हैं?	Which men live in the village?
कौन-से लड़कों ने शीशा तोड़ दिया?	Which boys broke the mirror?
तुम ने कौन-सी औरतों से बातचीत की?	Which women did you talk to?

§ 164. Both कौन and कौन-सा can be doubled and in this case they have a distributive meaning:

मेरे साथ कौन कौन चलेगा?	Who [among you] will come with me?
मन्दिर में कौन कौन थे?	Which ones were in the temple?
आप किन किन-से बातचीत करेंगे?	Which ones will you speak to?

§ 165. क्या "what? which?" refers to inanimates and is used both independently and as a modifier:

यह क्या है?	What is this?
आप हिन्दी में यह क्या कहते हैं?	What do you call this in Hindī?
तुम ने क्या किया है?	What have you done?
क्या बात है?	What's the matter?

§ 166. The oblique case of क्या coincides with the oblique sing. of कौन:

वे किस के बारे में बोल रहे थे?	What were they talking about? or: Whom were they talking about?

§ 167. काहे is another, less common and archaic oblique form of क्या:

यह काहे का बना है? or: यह किस का बना है?	What is this made of?

§ 168. क्या can be doubled, in which case it has a distributive meaning:

तुम क्या क्या लाए?	What [different things] did you bring?
स्टेशन पर क्या क्या चीज़ें बिकती हैं?	What [different] things are sold at the station?

§ 169. क्या is commonly used as a pure question-marker. When used in this way, it is placed first in the sentence and is **not** translated:

क्या मोहन आ गया?	Did Mohan come?
क्या मैं यहाँ बैठूँ?	May I sit down here?

§ 170. क्या is used emphatically in exclamations:

क्या सुन्दर लड़की!	What a beautiful girl!
क्या अच्छा! क्या अच्छी बात!	How nice! How nice!

INDEFINITE PRONOUNS.

§ 171. There are two main indefinite pronouns in Hindī: कोई "someone, some" and कुछ "something, some". Both are used as A. independent pronouns, and B. modifiers to nouns. The paradigm is:

	Sing.		Plur.	
Dir.	कोई	कुछ	(कोई)	कुछ
Obl.	किसी	कुछ	(कोई)	कुछ

§ 172. Independent कोई:

कोई आ रहा है.	Someone is coming.
क्या कोई यहाँ है?	Is there anyone here?
कोई पेड़ के नीचे बैठा हुआ है.	Someone is sitting under the tree.
मैं पेड़ के नीचे किसी को देख रहा हूँ.	I see someone under the tree.
मैं किसी की आवाज़ सुन रहा हूँ.	I hear someone's voice.

§ 173. As modifier to a noun कोई means "some[body], a certain'. It is commonly used as an indefinite article. See § 73.

कोई बच्चा रो रहा है.	Some/A child is crying.
कोई लड़की पानी लाएगी.	Some/A girl will bring water.

कोई पुस्तक मेज़ पर पड़ी है.	There is a book lying on the table.
कोई चीज़ कोने में है.	There is something in the corner.
किसी नगर में कोई अमीर सेठ रहता था.	In a town there lived a rich merchant.
आप किसी बच्चे से पूछ सकते हैं.	You can ask some/a child.

§ 174. Plural कोई is invariable and always used as a modifier:

कोई बच्चे बाग में खेल रहे हैं.	Some children are playing in the garden.
कोई औरतें कपड़े धो रही हैं.	Some women are washing clothes.
लड़का कोई लड़कियों के साथ खेलना नहीं चाहता.	The boy does not want to play with any girls.
उस ने कोई लोगों को बाग में देखा.	He saw some people in the garden.

§ 175. The plural can also be expressed by कोई-कोई, which can be used both independently or as a modifier:

कोई कोई (लोग) आ रहे हैं.	Some (people) are coming.

§ 176. Another way of conveying an indefinite plural is the pronoun कई "some, many". If used independently it has the oblique case कइयों :

कई किताबें मेज़ पर पड़ी थीं.	Some/Several books were lying on the table.

§ 177. कोई before numerals means "approximately" (cf. § 264):

कोई पन्द्रह आदमी.	About fifteen men.
कोई दस मिनट के बाद.	After approximately ten minutes.

§ 178. कोई + a negative means "nobody, nothing" = "not anybody, not anything":

गाँव में कोई तालाब नहीं है.	There is no watertank in the village.
मकान के पीछे कोई नहीं.	There is nobody behind the house.
मैं ने किसी आदमी को नहीं देखा.	I did not see any man.
कोई बात नहीं.	It doesn't matter.

वह कोई किताब नहीं पढ़ रहा था. He wasn't reading any book.
मैं कोई औरतों से बातचीत करने के लिए तैयार नहीं हूँ. I am not prepared to talk to any women.

§ 179. As the paradigm shows, कुछ is invariable:

कुएँ में कुछ है. There is something in the well.
क्या घर में कुछ खाना है? Is there any food in the house?
कुछ लड़कियाँ कपड़े धो रही हैं. Some girls are washing clothes.
कुछ बच्चे पेड़ों के नीचे बैठे हैं. Some children are sitting under the trees.
मैं कुछ किताबें खरीदूँगा. I'll buy some books.
कुछ ऐसे होते हैं. Some [people] are like that.
कुछ की भाषा सहज होती है. The language of some [people] is simple.

§ 180. कुछ + a negative means "nothing" = "not anything":

मैं इस के बारे में कुछ नहीं जानता. I know nothing about this.
उस ने बाग में कुछ नहीं देखा. He did not see anything in the garden.

§ 181. From the above examples it is clear that कोई and कुछ may be used in very similar contexts. Both can be used with reference to both animate beings and inanimate objects. The difference is that कोई refers to a particular person or thing, while कुछ is general. Compare the following examples:

कोई साधू बाहर खड़ा है. There is a sādhū standing outside.
कुछ साधू नदी में नहा रहे हैं. Some sādhūs are bathing in the river.
गाँव में कोई नाई नहीं है. There is no barber in the village.
तालाब में कुछ पानी नहीं है. There is no water in the tank.

OTHER INDEFINITE PRONOUNS.

§ 182. दूसरा "other", और "other", "another", बहुत "many" are also indefinite pronouns. They are used both as independent pronouns and as modifiers to nouns. When used independently in the plural they have the ending -ओं in the oblique case :

दूसरों की आँखों में	In the eyes of others...
दूसरे लोग आ चुके थे.	Other people had already come.
औरों के सामने	In front of others...
और लोगों के सामने	In front of other people...
बहुत लोग आ गए थे.	Many people had come.
बहुतों की आँखों में	In the eyes of many...

§ 183. सब "all, everyone" is an indefinite pronoun expressing totality. It is usually invariable, but when it is used independently in the oblique plural it may take the form सभों, or sometimes सबों :

सब लोग ऐसे होते हैं.	Everyone is like that.
सब/सभों के लिए.	For everyone.

COMPOUND INDEFINITE PRONOUNS.

§ 184. कोई can be combined in different ways to express "someone else, another": कोई और obl. किसी और, और कोई obl. और किसी, कोई दूसरा obl. किसी दूसरे. In this context और is always stressed. Examples:

वह मोहन नहीं था, कोई और था.	That wasn't Mohan, it was someone else.
और कोई नहीं आया.	No-one else came.
किसी और को दे दीजिए.	Give [it] to someone else!
किसी दूसरे ने किया होगा.	Someone else must have done [it].

§ 185. Similarly कुछ और, और कुछ "something further, something different, some more":

और कुछ चाहिये.	Do you want anything else?
कुछ और लीजिये.	Take a little more, please!

§ 186. कोई–न–कोई "someone or other" :

घर में कोई न कोई अवश्य होगा.	There must be someone or other in the house.

§187. कोई ... कोई "some ... others":

कोई आ रहे हैं, कोई जा रहे हैं.	Some are coming, others are going.

§ 188. कुछ न कुछ "something or other":

हम कुछ न कुछ कर लेंगे.	We'll do something or other.

§ 189. कुछ-का-कुछ "something entirely different":

कुछ का कुछ हो गया.	Something totally different happened.

§ 190. कुछ कुछ "somewhat, a little":

मुझे कुछ कुछ बुख़ार है.	I have a little fever.

§ 191. बहुत कुछ "a large amount, a lot":

उस को बहुत कुछ मालूम है.	He knows a lot.

§ 192. सब कुछ "everything":

उस ने जुए में सब कुछ उड़ा दिया.	He squandered everything gambling.

§ 193. Further possibilities to express totality are सब कोई "all, everyone", हर कोई, हरेक, प्रत्येक "everyone, each":

सब कोई जानता है कि वह दूकानदार बहुत बेईमान है.
Everyone knows that that shopkeeper is very dishonest.

हरेक आदमी को ऐसा मौका नहीं मिलता.
Not everyone gets such an opportunity.

RELATIVE PRONOUNS.

§ 194. The relative pronoun जो has the following paradigm:

	Sing.	Pl.
Dir.	जो	जो
Obl. + ने	जिस ने	जिन्हों ने
Obl.	जिस	जिन
Spec. object form	जिसे	जिन्हें

§ 195. In Hindī, the relative clause normally **precedes** the correlative clause which refers back to the relative clause through the demonstrative pronoun वह:

जो उस ने कहा वह सच है. — What he said [that] is true.

जिसे तुम ने देखा वह बीमार था. — The man you saw was ill. (Lit. Whom you saw he was ill.)

§ 196. Normally the relative pronoun modifies a noun which is referred back to by the demonstrative pronoun in the main clause:

जो खाना आप ने मेरे लिये पकाया, वह बहुत अच्छा था.
The food which you cooked for me was very good.

जो आदमी खेत पर काम कर रहा है, वह मेरा भाई है.
The man who is working in the field is my brother.

जो पानी नदी से आता है, उसे मैं नहीं पी सकता.
I cannot drink the water that comes from the river.

जिस नदी में हम तैरते थे, वह बहुत गहरी थी.
The river in which we used to swim was very deep.

जिन औरतों ने खाना पकाया, उन्हों ने उसे नहीं खाया.
The women who cooked the food did not eat it.

जिस आदमी ने यह मेज़ बनाई है, वह बहुत अच्छा बढ़ई है.
The man who has made this table is a very good carpenter.

§ 197. The relative clause may follow the correlative as in English. In these cases the relative pronoun is **independent**:

वह औरत जो घर के सामने बैठी हुई है मेरी माँ है.
The woman who is sitting in front of the house is my mother.

उस किताब को जो मेज़ पर पड़ी थी मैं लाया हूँ.
I have brought the book which was lying on the table.

वह कुर्सी जिस की मरम्मत तुम ने की कहाँ है?
Where is the chair which you repaired?

वह आदमी जिसे मैं ने बाहर देखा मज़दूर है.
The man whom I saw outside is a workman.

वे औरतें जिन से हम बातचीत कर रहे थे आगरे से आई हैं.
The women with whom we were talking have come from Āgrā.

§ 198. The archaic demonstrative pronoun सो replaces वह in proverbs and idiomatic expressions:

जो होगा सो होगा. — What will be will be.

जो गरजते हैं सो बरसते नहीं. — Those [clouds] that thunder do not rain. (= His bark is worse than his bite.)

§ 199. सो has the seldom used oblique forms तिस (sg.) and तिन (pl.):

जिस की लाठी तिस की भैंस. — Might is right. (Lit. He who has the stick has the buffalo.)

INDEFINITE RELATIVE PRONOUNS.

§ 200. The relative pronoun जो can be combined with
1. itself : जो जो
2. the indefinite pronouns कोई and कुछ: जो कोई, जो कुछ
3. the emphatic particle भी: जो भी

to express "whoever, whatever". The emphatic particle भी can also be added to 1 and 2 above (cf. § 441) :

जो जो चाहिये मिलेगा. — Whatever is necessary will be available.

जो कोई आए उसे यह ख़ब्र दीजिए. — Whoever comes, give him this news!

मन्दिर में जो कोई आए उसे खाना खिलाओ.
Feed whoever comes into the temple.

जो कोई भी देवताओं का मित्र हो वह हमारी रक्षा करे. Whoever is the friend of the gods, may he protect us.

जो कुछ मिले रख लो! Keep whatever you get!

जो भी औरत पानी लाई वह घर में घुसी होगी. Whichever woman brought the water must have entered the house.

जिस ने भी यह किया वह मूर्ख है. Whoever did this is a fool.

§ 201. In the oblique case **both pronouns** are declined:

जिस किसी का घर भी हो उसे जला दो. Burn the house down, whoever owns it!

जिस किसी ने यह किया वह मूर्ख है. Whoever did this is a fool.

ADJECTIVES.

§ 202. There are two types of adjectives in Hindī:

1. Gender-Number-marked adjectives; and
2. Unmarked adjectives.

§ 203. Gender-Number-marked adjectives always have the lexical form ending in –आ, i.e. masc. sing. : छोटा "small, young", काला "black".

Paradigm पीला "yellow":

	Sing.	Pl.
Masc. dir.	पीला	पीले
Masc. obl.	पीले	पीले
Fem. dir.	पीली	पीली
Fem. obl.	पीली	पीली

Note that the feminine always ends in –ई, regardless of number or case.

§ 204. If a GN-marked adjective is nasalized it keeps the nasalization all through the paradigm. All ordinal numbers from 7th onward are nasalized, and so is पाँचवाँ "fifth": सातवाँ, सातवीं, सातवें "seventh".

§ 205. Unmarked adjectives end either in a consonant, i.e. with inherent, unpronounced –अ (see § 23.1), or in –ई or –ऊ. They remain unchanged all through the paradigm.

§ 206. Adjectives occur in both attributive and predicative position:

छोटा बच्चा सो रहा है.	The little child is sleeping.
मेरे पास दो नए रूमाल हैं.	I have two new handkerchiefs.
काली पेंसिलें मेज़ पर पड़ी हैं.	The black pencils are lying on the table.
वह उस पीले घर में रहता है.	He lives in that yellow house.
छोटी लड़की गुड़िया लाई.	The little girl brought a doll.
उसे साफ़ कमीज़ दे दो!	Give him a clean shirt!
ऊपरवाला कमरा खाली है.	The upstairs room is vacant.
यह कपड़ा बहुत सस्ता है.	This cloth is very cheap.

यह दुकान बड़ी अच्छी है.	This shop is very good.
दिल्ली के मकान काफ़ी ऊँचे हैं.	The houses in Delhi are rather high.
हमारी लड़कियाँ छोटी हैं.	Our daughters are young.
औरतें खुबसूरत हैं.	The women are beautiful.
मेरी नई साड़ी लाल है.	My new saree is red.

§ 207. Some adjectives in -आ are unmarked. These adjectives are always of Persian-Arabic origin. Since Urdū has a larger number of Persian-Arabic loanwords, it consequently has more unmarked adjectives in -आ than Standard Hindī: ज़िन्दा "alive", मादा "female", पैदा "born", बेजा "out of place, improper", आवारा "vagrant".

सीता ज़िन्दा है.	Sītā is alive.
उन को लड़की पैदा हुई.	They got a girl. (Lit. A girl was born to them.)
मेरी बातें बेजा नहीं थीं.	My words were not improper.
ये गलियों के आवारा बेकार कुत्ते ...	These straying idle alley-dogs ...

§ 208. Standard Hindī has a tendency to regularize these unmarked adjectives in -आ, so that they sometimes are Gender-Number-marked:

वह रोज़ ताज़ा सब्ज़ियाँ / ताज़ी सब्ज़ियाँ खरीदती है.	She buys fresh vegetables every day.
आँगन में कोई चालीस आदमी इकट्ठा / इकट्ठे थे.	Some forty men were assembled in the courtyard.

§ 209. The Hindī adjective in attributive position normally precedes the noun it qualifies, as shown in the above examples. However, in elegant Persianized Urdū the adjective as attribute is sometimes postposited and linked by an "ezāfeh" which is written in Devanāgarī script either as -इ- or as -ए- (in this particular case -ए- is always pronounced short):
दिवान-इ-ख़ास the special (private) audience hall
दिवान-ए-आम the common audience hall

§ 210. Adjectives used as adverbs, see §§ 236-239.

§ 211. All adjectives may be used as nouns; when they are used as nouns, they are treated as such, i.e. they follow the nominal declensions (see §§ 33-34, 36-37, 39) काला "the black [one]", लाल "the red [one]":

	Sing.		Plur.	
Masc. dir.	काला	लाल	काले	लाल
obl.	काले	लाल	कालों	लालों
Fem. dir.	काली	लाल	कालियाँ	लालें
obl.	काली	लाल	कालियों	लालों

अन्धों में काना राजा.	Among the blind the one-eyed is king.
काँग्रस गरीबों की पर्टी है.	Congress is the party of the poor.

§ 212. Adjectives are frequently used as nouns in neologisms such as समाजवादी "socialist", आतंकवादी "terrorist", विचारवादी "idealist", विधायक "legislator".

COMPARISON.

§ 213. The Hindī adjective has no separate forms to mark the comparative and the superlative. These degrees are expressed through special syntactic constructions.

§ 214. The comparative is expressed by putting that which is being compared in the oblique case followed by the postposition से:

मदन राम से बड़ा है.	Madan is bigger than Rām.
पेड़ मकानों से ऊँचे हैं.	The trees are higher than the houses.
यह साड़ी उस से सस्ती है.	This saree is cheaper than that one.

§ 215. In more formal discourse, से may be replaced by expressions meaning "in comparison with", such as

X की अपेक्षा
X की तुलना में

X की निसबत — in comparison with X, than X
X के बनिसबत
X के मुकाबले, मुकाबिले में

दाहिना फेफड़ा बाएँ फेफड़े की अपेक्षा चौड़ा और भारी होता है.
The right lung is bigger and heavier than the left lung.

§ 216. से may be reinforced with the absolutive बढ़कर,बढ़के with the meaning "more, better than, superior to":

माँ से बढ़कर कोई गुरु नहीं. — No teacher is better than mother.

§ 217. कहीं may precede the adjective to underline the comparative:

यह कहीं अच्छा है. — This is much better.

§ 218. If that which is being compared is left unexpressed, the adjective is preceded by a stressed और or और भी:

और बड़ा संदूक लाओ! — Bring a bigger box!
सीता बहुत सुन्दर है, लेकिन उस की बहिन और भी सुन्दर है.
Sītā is very beautiful, but her sister is even more beautiful.

§ 219. The superlative is indicated by सब से, literally "than all" which in this context functions as a superlative marker and is mostly left untranslated:

तुम सब से बड़े हो. — You are the biggest [of all].
वह पेड़ सब से ऊँचा है. — That tree is highest.
दुनिया के सब से अमीर आदमी यहाँ रहते हैं.
The richest men in the world live here.

§ 220. If the object of comparison is being expressed, Hindī uses से, में or both में and से:

तारा सब लड़कियों (में) से सुन्दर है.
Tārā is the most beautiful among the girls.
[Tārā is the most beautiful girl.]

तुम सब मित्रों में (से) अच्छे हो. You are the best friend.
सीता उन औरतों में से बूढ़ी है. Sītā is the oldest of these women.

§ 221. The superlative may also be expressed by repeating the same adjective before से or में :

बड़े से बड़ा होटल the biggest hotel
अच्छे से अच्छा मित्र the best friend

§ 222. Both the comparative and the superlative may be reinforced by suitable adverbs such as अधिक or ज़्यादा:

यह साड़ी उस से ज़्यादा सस्ती है. This saree is cheaper than that one.
यह तसवीर सब से ज़्यादा सस्ता है. This picture is cheapest.
पिताजी सब से अधिक बुद्धिमान हैं. Father is wisest [of all].

§ 223. In formal discourse, the Sanskrit comparative suffix -तर and the superlative suffix -तम may occur:

उच्चतर "higher", पुण्यतर "holier",
प्रियतम "dear, dearest', आधुनिकतम "most modern".

Note that if a Sanskrit suffix is added, the adjective keeps its *tatsam* form: उच्च, not ऊँचा.

§ 224. Some Sanskrit superlatives in -(इ)ष्ठ have survived, not always in a strict superlative sense:

श्रेष्ठ "very good, best, excellent", सर्वश्रेष्ठ "most excellent", बलिष्ठ "very strong", कनिष्ठ "younger, youngest", ज्येष्ठ "older, oldest"; note also the fake Sanskrit superlative घनिष्ठ "closest, most intimate".

§ 225. A limited number of Persian comparatives and superlatives are relatively common, such as बेहतर "better", बेहतरीन "best", बदतर "worse", ज़्यादातर "most, often":

आप को उस दुकान में हिन्दुस्तान का बेहतरीन कपड़ा मिलेगा.
You will get the best cloth in India in this shop.

ADVERBS.

§ 226. There are several types of adverbs in Hindī:

1. Lexical adverbs
2. other classes of words such as adjectives used as adverbs (see §§ 236 ff.), nouns used in periphrastic formations (see §§ 229-234 below), absolutives, participles, etc. which can function as adverbs.

§ 227. Lexical adverbs are

A. all pronominal adverbs, see §§ 240-245

B. words that are exclusively defined as adverbs in a dictionary, such as हमेशा "always", आज "today", फ़ौरन "immediately", etc.

आजकल मक्खन बहुत महँगा है.	Butter is very expensive nowadays.
वह हमेशा खुश है.	He is always happy.
लड़कियाँ एक साथ खेल रही हैं.	The girls are playing together.
पत्नी फ़ौरन चाय लाई.	The wife brought tea immediately.
आदमी बाहर काम करते हैं.	The men work outside.

C. The adverbs of negation are नहीं, न, and मत. नहीं is the most common negation for all tenses in the indicative mood, but न may alternate with नहीं (see § 314) and is obligatory in contrary-to-fact statements (see §§ 338-340). न is obligatory in the subjunctive mood, and alternates with मत in the imperative mood:

वह नहीं आया.	He did not come.
बारिश न हो रही होती तो...	If it were not raining ...
झूठ मत बोलो!	Don't lie!

§ 228. Some adverbs of time are ambiguous and get their meaning from the tense of the finite verb:

कल	yesterday, tomorrow
परसों	day before yesterday, day after tomorrow
तरसों	three days ago, in three days
नरसों	four days ago, in four days
वह कल आया.	He came yesterday.
वह कल आएगा.	He'll come tomorrow.
बस नरसों छूटेगी.	The bus will leave in four days.
वह नरसों चली गई.	She left four days ago.

OTHER ADVERBS AND ADVERBIAL PHRASES.

§ 229. Adverbs of time, place and manner are normally formed by a noun + postposition, cf. POSTPOSITIONS §§ 81.6, 83.4, 84.1, 85.1, 86-93.

नौकर जल्दी से चाय ला रहा है.	The servant brings tea quickly.
उस ने क्रोध में कहा...	He said angrily...
दूसरों की बात सब्र से सुननी चाहिये.	One should listen to others patiently.
शाम को वापस आएगा.	He'll return in the evening.
इतवार को हम शहर जाते हैं.	We go to the town on Sundays.

§ 230. The postposition is often omitted, especially if the noun is modified:

अगले महीने वह वापस आएगी.	She'll return next month.
कल रात दंगा हुआ.	There was a riot last night.
इन दिनों मौसम बहुत ठण्डा है.	These days the weather is very cold.
अन्धेरे में थोड़ी देर रहा.	He remained in the darkness for a short while.
चोर दबे पाँव मकान में घुस आया.	The thief entered the house tip-toeing/stealthily.

§ 231. Adverbs can be formed by an adjective + a noun meaning "way, kind, manner" such as तौर, ढंग, रीति, तरह, भाव, रूप + a postposition, generally से or पर:

आम तौर पर	generally
ऐच्छिक तौर से	voluntarily
ऐतिहासिक ढंग से	historically
गुप्त रीति से	secretly
अधिकार के भाव से	with authority, in an authoritarian way
शान्त रूप से	quietly, peacefully

§ 232. When तरह is used the postposition is generally omitted:

अच्छी तरह	well
इस तरह	in this way
हर तरह	in every way
किसी न किसी तरह	somehow, in some way or other

§ 233. Adverbs may be formed by adding the suffixes भर or मात्र to a noun:

वह रात भर काम करता है.	He works all night.
तुम दिन भर कहाँ रहे?	Where were you all day?
क्षण मात्र यहाँ रुको!	Stop here for a moment!

§ 234. Adverbs may be formed by an adjective + the absolutive होकर :

सशङ्क होकर	suspiciously
मज़बूर होकर	forcedly, necessarily

§ 235. Regarding adverbially used absolutives, see § 413.

ADJECTIVES AS ADVERBS.

§ 236. Any adjective can be used as an adverb. Its syntactic function in these cases is either as adverb of manner, place or time or as subjective or objective completion.

§ 237. Unmarked adjectives always stay the same, as in

मैं चुप रही.	I remained silent.
वह अवाक बुढ़िया को देखती रही.	Speechless, she kept looking at the old woman.
उस ने अपना कमरा साफ़ किया.	He cleaned his room. (Lit. He made his room clean.)

§ 238. If the adjective is GN-marked, there are three possibilities:

1. the adjective is in masc. sing. obl. case, regardless of the number and the gender of the main word. This seems to be the most commonly used way:

बन्दर पेड़ से नीचे आ रहा है.	The monkey is coming down from the tree.
पहले मैं गाँव में रहती थी.	I lived in a village before.
आदमी धीरे-धीरे बोल रहा है.	The man is speaking very slowly.
बाएँ जाइए!	Please go to the left!

भागीरथ सीधे अपने घर चला गया। Bhāgīrath went straight home.
राम ने वन में सीता को अकेले छोड़ दिया।
Rām abandoned Sītā alone in the forest.
मैं ने एक स्त्री को वहाँ खड़े पाया। I found a woman standing there.

2. the adjective agrees with its main word, whether it is in a position of subjective or objective completion:

सीता सीधी चली, फिर दाहिने। Sītā went straight, then to the right.
मुझे अकेली रहने में डर नहीं लगता। I am not afraid to live alone (said by a woman).
क्या उसे आशा थी कि वह शारदा को द्वार पर खड़ी पाएगा।
Had he hoped to find Śārdā standing at the door?
यहाँ गाड़ी खड़ी न करें। You may not park the car here.
आँखें नीची किये उन की बातें सुनता रहा।
He kept listening to their talk, his eyes lowered.

3. The adjective remains in masc. sing. direct case, regardless of the number and gender of the main word:

आप बहुत अच्छा खेलती हैं, मिस शर्मा।
You play very well, Miss Śarmā.
नहीं, आप मुझ से अाच्छा खेलते हैं। No, you play better than me.
छोटे बच्चों को अकेला नहीं छोड़ना चाहिये।
Small children should not be left alone.
वह किसी भी पुरुष से अपने को छोटा नहीं समझती थी।
She did not consider herself inferior to any man.
दो पुलिसियों ने छह बच्चों को नंगा करके डंडों से पीटा।
Two policemen stripped and beat up six children with sticks.

§ 239. Adverbially used participles behave in an analogous manner, see § 382.

PRONOMINAL ADJECTIVES AND ADVERBS.

§ 240. A certain number of adjectives and adverbs are related to demonstrative, relative and interrogative pronouns:

	Demonstrative		Relative	Interrogative
Quantity	इतना	उतना	जितना	कितना
	this much	that much	[as much] as	how much?
Quality	ऐसा	वैसा	जैसा	कैसा
	this sort	that sort	as, like	what sort?
Time	अब	तब	जब	कब
	now	then	when	when?
Place	यहाँ	वहाँ	जहाँ	कहाँ
	here	there	where	where?
Direction	इधर	उधर	जिधर	किधर
	hither	thither	whither	whither?
Manner	यों	त्यों	ज्यों	क्यों
	like this	like that	as, as if	why?

§ 241. As question-marker the pronominal adverb क्या is never translated into English (see § 169) :

क्या वे तुम्हारे बड़े भाई हैं? Is he your elder brother?

§ 242. The pronominal adjectives इतना, उतना, जितना, कितना and ऐसा, वैसा, जैसा, कैसा are GN-marked:

जितनी किताबें चाहते हो, उतने खरीद लो!
Buy as many books as you want!

तुम ने कितने पैसे दिये? How much did you pay?

ऐसी बात मत करो! Don't talk like this!

§ 243. The pronominal adjectives, like all other adjectives, can be used as adverbs:

यह कैसा हुआ? How did this happen?

कौन ऐसा करेगा? Who would do such [a thing]?

वह इतना रोया कि मेरा दिल टूट गया.
He wept so much that my heart broke.

कैसे उधर जा सकता हूँ? How can I go there?

क्या तू चाहता है कि मैं ऐसे ही मर जाऊँ?
Do you wish that I may die just like this?

Note the expression ऐसा लगता है कि it seems that …

§ 244. The emphatic particle ही (see § 440) can be added to all pronominal adjectives and adverbs. Note the spelling in the following cases: अभी, तभी, जभी, कभी and यहीं (from यहाँ+ही), वहीं, जहीं, कहीं.

Note: कभी and कहीं are not emphatic interrogative adverbs, but indefinite adverbs: कभी "sometime, ever", कहीं "somewhere, anywhere":

क्या आप कभी बम्बई गए हैं? Have you ever been to Bombay?
उस ने मुझे चिट्ठी कभी नहीं लिखी. He never wrote a letter to me.
वह कहीं गया है. He has gone somewhere.

§ 245. Pronominal adverbs can be followed by a postposition or the genitive marker का:

अब से	from now
तब तक	up to then
कब से	since when?
कहाँ से	from where?
यहाँ तक	up to here
तब का	of then, of that time
यहाँ के खिलौने	the toys [that belong] here

NUMERALS.

§ 246. Hindī numerals can be divided into three main groups:

1. Cardinals,
2. Ordinals,
3. Fractional numbers.

CARDINALS.

§ 247. **Cardinals** are learnt most easily by starting from 1-9, then learning them by tens from ten to one hundred, and finally learning the allophones for each number up to ten. Cardinals are invariable.

§ 248. 1/१ एक 2/२ दो 3/३ तीन 4/४ चार 5/५ पाँच 6/६ छः 7/७ सात 8/८ आठ 9/९ नौ

§ 249. 10/१० दस 20/२० बीस 30/३० तीस 40/४० चालीस 50/५० पचास 60/६० साठ 70/७० हत्तर 80/८० अस्सी 90/९० नब्बे 100/१०० सौ

§ 250. एक "one", allophone इक, इक्या, exception ग्यारह "eleven":

1 एक	11 ग्यारह	21 इक्कीस	31 इकत्तीस	41 इकतालीस
51 इक्यावन	61 इकसठ	71 इकहत्तर	81 इक्यासी	91 इक्यानवे

§ 251. दो "two" allophone बा, ब:

2 दो	12 बारह	22 बाईस	32 बत्तीस	42 बयालीस
52 बावन	62 बासठ	72 बहत्तर	82 बयासी	92 बानवे

Note the glide -य- in बयालीस and बयासी.

§ 252. तीन "three", allophones ते, तैं, तिर, ति:

3 तीन	13 तेरह	23 तेईस	33 तैंतीस	43 तैंतालीस
53 तिरपन	63 तिरसठ	73 तिहत्तर	83 तिरासी	93 तिरानवे

§ 253. चार "four", allophones चौ, चव, चौं, चौर :

4 चार	14 चौदह	24 चौबीस	34 चौंतीस	44 चवालीस
54 चौवन	64 चौंसठ	74 चौहत्तर	84 चौरासी	94 चौरानवे

§ 254. पाँच "five", allophones पच, पचा, पैं, exception पन्द्रह "fifteen":

5 पाँच	15 पन्द्रह	25 पच्चीस	35 पैंतीस	45 पैंतालीस
55 पचपन	65 पैंसठ	75 पचहत्तर	85 पचासी	95 पचानवे

§ 255. छह (छः, छै) "six", allophones छि, छ , exception सोलह "sixteen":

6 छह	16 सोलह	26 छब्बीस	36 छत्तीस	46 छियालीस
56 छप्पन	66 छियासठ	76 छिहत्तर	86 छियासी	96 छियानवे

§ 256. सात "seven", allophones सत, सत्त, सैं, सर:

7 सात	17 सत्तरह	27 सत्ताईस	37 सैंतीस	47 सैंतालीस
57 सत्तावन	67 सरसठ	77 सतहत्तर	87 सत्तासी	97 सत्तानवे

§ 257. आठ "eight", allophones अट्ट, अड़, अठ:

8 आठ	18 अठारह	28 अट्ठाईस	38 अड़तीस	48 अड़तालीस
58 अट्ठावन	68 अड़सठ	78 अठहत्तर	88 अठासी	98 अट्ठानवे

§ 258. नौ "nine", has no allophones, except possibly नवासी and निन्यानवे "eighty nine" and "ninety nine". The rest of the cardinals which in English would end in "-nine" are formed as follows:

9 नौ	19 उन्नीस	29 उनतीस	39 उनतालीस	49 उनचास
59 उनसठ	69 उनहत्तर	79 उन्यासी (उन्नासी) and the exceptions		

89 नवासी and 99 निन्यानवे.

§ 259. Cardinals from 100 onwards are formed as follows:

100 सौ	200 दो सौ	300 तीन सौ
101 एक सौ एक	211 दो सौ ग्यारह	321 तीन सौ इक्कीस
102 एक सौ दो	212 दो सौ बारह	322 तीन सौ बाईस
103 एक सौ तीन	213 दो सौ तेरह	323 तीन सौ तेईस

1 000 १००० एक हज़ार/एक सहस्र 2 000 २००० दो हज़ार
2 478 २४७८ दो हज़ार चार सौ अठहत्तर
100 000 १,००,००० एक लाख २,००,००० दो लाख
१०,००,००० दस लाख (= 1 million)
१,००,००,००० एक करोड़ (= 10 millions)
१,००,००,००,००० एक अर्ब (अरब) (= one billion) 1 000 000 000

§ 260. It is normal in India to count large numbers in *lākh* and *karoṛ*. The sum 84, 567, 314 will read आठ करोड़ पैंतालीस लाख सरसठ हज़ार तीन सौ चौदह and is written 8,45,67,314.

§ 261. लाख and करोड़ are always preceded by a numeral, including एक. हज़ार and सहस्र can delete एक:

लड़ाई में एक लाख आदमी मर गये. 100 000 men died in the war.

§ 262. Zero is expressed by the nouns शून्य masc. or सिफ़र masc.

§ 263. Approximate numbers may be expressed by hyphenating two cardinal numbers, often in descending order, or adding एक:

दो चार टमाटर	a few (lit. two-four) tomatoes
दस पाँच आदमी	some (five-ten) men
बीस तीस कमीज़ें	twenty-thirty shirts
चार एक बजे	around four o'clock

Regarding the number of the noun after numerals see § 61.

§ 264. Approximate numbers may also be expressed through a preceding कोई (see § 177), लगभग, प्राय : or a postposited एक:

कोई पचास आदमी	around fifty men
लगभग पाँच सौ	about five hundred
प्राय : दो सौ वर्ष हुए	about two hundred years ago
सत्तरेक लड़के आ गये.	About seventy boys came.

§ 265. The ending -ओं added to cardinals implies inclusiveness: दोनों both, तीनों all three, चारों all four, etc.:

दोनों लड़के अच्छे थे.	Both the boys were nice.
गाँव के चारों ओर हरियाली ही हरियाली है.	All around (lit. in all four directions of) the village there is nothing but greenery.
चालीसों चोर गुफ़ा में घुस गए.	All the forty thieves entered the cave.

§ 266. -ओं can also be added to nouns: दरज़नों "dozens" from दरज़न masc. dozen; बीसियों "scores" from बीसी fem. score, a quantity of twenty, सैकड़ों hundreds" from सैकड़ा masc. a quantity of hundred, a century; हज़ारों "thousands", लाखों "hundreds of thousands".

सैकड़ों आदमी मर गए.	Hundreds of men died.

ORDINALS.

§ 267. Ordinals are GN-marked and are used as adjectives, and, in the case of दूसरा , as a pronoun:

पहला	first, the first	छठा	sixth, the sixth
दूसरा	second, the second, the other	सातवाँ	seventh, the seventh
तीसरा	third, the third	आठवाँ	eight, the eight
चौथा	fourth, the fourth	नवाँ	ninth, the ninth
पाँचवाँ	fifth, the fifth	दसवाँ	tenth, the tenth

§ 268. From सातवाँ "seventh" onward all cardinals are created by adding the GN-marked ending -वाँ to the cardinal number:

एक सौ एकवाँ	one hundred and first
तीन सौ दोवाँ	three hundred and second
दो सौ इक्कीसवाँ	two hundred and twenty first
तीन हज़ार सोलहवाँ	three thousand and sixteenth

§ 269. *tatsam* ordinals may occur, especially in the written language:

प्रथम	first	षष्ठ	sixth
द्वितीय	second	सप्तम	seventh
तृतीय	third	अष्टम	eighth
चतुर्थ	fourth	नवम	ninth
पँचम	fifth	दशम	tenth

§ 270. Hindu religious days are expressed through *tatsam* ordinals with a *tatsam* fem. ending:

अष्टमी (fem.) the eight day (of the lunar calendar)
एकदशी (fem.) the eleventh day (of the lunar calendar)

FRACTIONS.

§ 271. आधा "half" masc. or GN-marked adj. : उस का आधा half of that; आधी रात midnight; आधा प्याला half a cup; आधे प्याले half of the cups; आधी किताबें half of the books.

§ 272. डेढ़ masc. "one and a half" : डेढ़ रुपया a rupee and a half, i.e. 1 rup. 50 n.p.; डेढ़ सौ 150; डेढ़ हज़ार 1 500; डेढ़ लाख 150 000.

§ 273. ढाई masc. "two and a half": ढाई रुपये two rupees and a half, i.e. 2 rup. 50 n.p.; ढाई हज़ार 2 500; ढाई मील two and a half miles.

§ 274. तिहाई fem. "third [part]": तिहाई देश or देश की एक तिहाई one third of the country; उस की दो तिहाई two thirds of it.

§ 275. चौथाई fem. "quarter, fourth part": दूध की एक चौथाई one quarter of the milk.

§ 276. पाव masc. "quarter": पाव रुपया a quarter of a rupee, प्रान्त के तीन पाव three quarters of the region.

§ 277. साढ़े adj. "plus a half" always precedes the numeral: साढ़े तीन three and a half; साढ़े चार सौ 450; साढ़े सात बजे at seven thirty.

§ 278. पौन, पौना adj. "three-quarters": पौन/पौना रुपया three quarters of a rupee; पौन सेर चावल three quarters of a seer of rice.

§ 279. पौने adj.obl. (invariable) preceding a cardinal means minus a quarter: पौने पच्चीस 24 3/4; पौने तीन गज़ 2 3/4 yards, i.e. 2 yards and 27 inches; पौने पाँच लाख 475 000.

§ 280. **सवा** adj. or masc. (invariable) preceding a cardinal means plus a quarter:
सवा सौ 125; **सवा हज़ार** 1 250; **सवा चार बजे** at 4:15; **सवा सेर दूध** one and a quarter seer milk; **बाप सेर, बेटा सवा सेर** lit. the father [is] a seer, the son [is] a seer and a quarter, i.e. the son is worse than the father.

§ 281. In the *devanāgarī* script a quarter is indicated by the sign **।**, a half by **।।**, three quarters by **।।।**: ३।।। = 3 3/4; ४।। = 4 1/2.

§ 282. The GN-marked suffix **गुना** added to a cardinal number (or its allophone) implies multiplication: **दुगुना** or **दुना** "twice", **तिगुना** "thrice"; **चौगुना** "four times", **पचगुना** "five times"; **छैगुना** "six times", **सतगुना** "seven times", **अठगुना** "eight times", **नौगुना** "nine times", **दसगुना** "ten times", **सौगुना** "hundred times", etc.

§ 283. **-गुना** can also be added to fractional numbers: **सवा गुना** "one and a quarter times"; **डेढ़ गुना** one and a half times"; **ढाई गुना** "two and a half times".

§ 284. The decimal fraction or decimal point is expressed by the nouns **दशमलव** masc., **दशमिक** masc., or **दशमिक बिन्दु** masc. :

पाँच दशमलव सोलह	5.16 five point sixteen
चालीस दशमिक आठ	40.8 forty point eight

§ 285. Percent is expressed by **प्रतिशत**, **प्रति**, **सैकड़ा**, **फ़ीसद** or **फ़ीसदी**.

VERBS (क्रिया).

§ 286. A Hindī verb is either object-taking (सकर्मक क्रिया) or non-object-taking (अकर्मक क्रिया).
All object-taking verbs can be made causative (प्रेरणार्थक क्रिया).

§ 287. Most Hindī verbs come in phonetically and semantically related pairs:

A. non-object-taking/object-taking verbs. The phonetic changes follow regular patterns with either variations in the stem-vowel or an -आ added to the stem.
B. two related object-taking verbs (see § 289 below).
C. other verbs in -आना (see §§ 290-292 below).

§ 288. Group A. has the following phonetic changes in the stem
1. -अ /-आ, **2.** -इ /-ई, **3.** -इ /-ए (-ऐ), **4.** -उ /-ऊ, **5.** -उ /-ओ and, finally, **6.** -आ added to the stem.

1. -अ/-आ

Non-object-taking		Object-taking	
मरना	to die	मारना	to kill, beat
छपना	to be printed	छापना	to print
लदना	to be loaded	लादना	to load
फटना	to be torn, to split	फाड़ना	to tear, to split

2. -इ / -ई

पिटना	to be beaten	पीटना	to beat
खिंचना	to be dragged	खींचना	to drag

3. -इ / -ए (-ऐ)

दिखना	to be visible, to appear	देखना	to see
बिकना	to be sold, to sell	बेचना	to sell
घिरना	to be surrounded	घेरना	to surround

4. -उ /-ऊ

लुटना	to be robbed	लूटना	to rob, to loot

5. -उ /-ओ

रुकना	to stop	रोकना	to stop (something)
खुलना	to open	खोलना	to open (something)

फुटना	to burst, split	फोड़ना	to split (something)
धुलना	to be washed	धोना	to wash

6. -आ added to the stem

बनना	to be made	बनाना	to make
जलना	to burn	जलाना	to burn (something)
उठना	to rise	उठाना	to raise
जागना	to wake up	जगाना	to wake (someone)
सोना	to sleep	सुलाना	to put to sleep

Note: since the inserted -आ- is stressed any long stem-vowel is shortened.

§ 289. Group B: There are object-taking verbs that form second, semantically related object-taking verbs by adding -आ- to the stem. All these verbs imply perception, mental faculties, and ingestion. Note that a long stem-vowel is shortened (cf. above):

सुनना	to hear	सुनाना	to tell
देखना	to see	दिखाना	to show
समझना	to understand	समझाना	to explain
पढ़ना	to study	पढ़ाना	to teach
सीखना	to learn	सिखाना	to teach
बोलना	to speak	बुलाना	to call, to summon
पीना	to drink	पिलाना	to give to drink
खाना	to eat	खिलाना	to give to eat, to feed

§ 290. There are verbs in -आना which are not the object-taking member of a pair. These are verbs derived from nouns and adjectives. They can be either non-object-taking (अकर्मक क्रिया) or object-taking (सकर्मक क्रिया) : लजाना (अ) "to be ashamed" from लज्जा f. "shame, embarrassment", सुस्ताना (अ) "to rest" from the adjective सुस्त "idle", बताना (स)"to tell" from बात, कमाना (स) "to earn" from काम "work, task", etc.

§ 291. Another category of verbs in -आना are the onomatopoeic verbs. These are usually created according to the following principle: reduplication of the stem + -आना : हिनहिनाना "to neigh", मिमियाना "to bleat", खटखटाना "to knock", etc. Most verbs in this category reproduce a sound of one kind or another. They are normally non-object-taking (अकर्मक क्रिया).

§ 292. Finally, there are some causative verbs in -आना, the most notable being कराना from करना. See § 364.

ASPECT, TENSE, VOICE AND MOOD .

§ 293. The Hindī verb has

1. two voices: active and passive;
2. three moods: indicative, subjunctive, and imperative;
3. three aspects: imperfective-habitual, progressive-continuous, and perfective;
4. two basic tenses: present and past, further subdivided according to aspects.

THE MORPHOLOGY OF THE VERB.

§ 294. The lexical form of the Hindi verb is characterized by the infinitive-marker -ना added to the verbal stem: कर-ना, सुन-ना, बोल-ना.
This form is called infinitive, but is in fact a verbal noun describing the action: चलना "going, the act of going", देखना "seeing, the act of seeing", रोना "weeping, the act of weeping". See §§ 388 ff.

§ 295. The verbal system is based on the stem to which different sets of markers are added:

1. Aspect-markers: -त्-, -Ø- (zero marker), and रह्-
The aspect-markers -त्- and -Ø- are added directly to the stem, the aspect-marker रह्- follows the short absolutive (see § 406).
2. The aspect-markers are followed by G(ender)-N(umber)-markers:
-आ (masc. sing.), -ए (masc. plur.), -ई fem. sing.), and -ई/ईं (fem. plur.).

Note: the nasalized fem. pl. occurs only in absolute final position, i.e. when not followed by any other verbal form.

3. There are two sets of P(erson)-N(umber)-markers: one for the subjunctive system and the other for the imperative system.

A. The subjunctive PN-markers are:

	Sing.	Plur.
1st person:	-ऊँ	-एँ
2nd person:	-ए	-ओ
3rd person:	-ए	-एँ

B. The PN-markers for the imperative system are:

	Sing.	Plur.
2nd person:	-Ø-	-ओ (-ना)
3rd person:	void	-इये (-इयेगा)

The P(erson)-N(umber)-markers are attached directly to the stem, without any intervening aspect-marker. Regarding the forms -ना and -इयेगा see §§ 356, 360, 361.

THE ASPECT-MARKER -त्-.

§ 296. The aspect-marker -त्-, added to the stem, indicates that the action is HABITUAL and IMPERFECTIVE (incomplete). By adding the GN-markers to the aspect-marker -त्- we obtain the IMPERFECTIVE PARTICIPLE: चलता "going", देखता "seeing", करता "doing". The imperfective participle is ACTIVE. The imperfective participle can be used as an adjective and as an adverb. See §§ 377 ff.

THE ASPECT-MARKER रह्-.

§ 297. The progressive aspect indicates that the action is continuous and progressive. It is created by combining the short absolutive (identical in form to the stem) + the GN-marked perfective participle रहा. However, for all practical purposes, रह्- can be considered a progressive aspect-marker in this combination. Note that रह्- is written separately from the main verb. Regarding the progressive participle see §§ 377-380.

THE ASPECT-MARKER -Ø- .

§ 298. The aspect-marker -Ø- added to the stem indicates that the action is perfective (completed) and not habitual. By adding the GN-markers to the zero marker we obtain the PERFECTIVE PARTICIPLE: चला "gone", देखा "seen", सुना "heard". The perfective participle is PASSIVE.
The perfective participle can be used as an adjective and an adverb.
See §§ 378 ff.

§ 299. **Morpho-phonemic rules relevant to the zero aspect-marker.** Since the zero marker is by definition mute and always followed by a vocalic GN-marker, certain phonetic changes occur if the stem ends in a vowel other than the inherent -अ-:

1. If the stem ends in -आ,-ए , or -ओ, the glide -य- is inserted before the GN-marker. This is compulsory if the GN-marker is -आ (masc. sing.), optional (but frequent) if the GN-marker is -ए (masc. pl.) or -ई (fem. sg. or pl.): खाया, लाया, खेया, धोया, but खाये or खाए , लाये or लाए , धोयी or धोई.

2. If the stem ends in -ई, the glide -य- is inserted before -आ and the stem-vowel is shortened: पिया (stem पी-). Before -ए the glide is optional, but the stem-vowel remains shortened: पिये or पिए . Before –ई, there is a contraction: पी (from पि-य्-ई) (cf. DECLENSION §§ 35, 37).

3. If the stem ends in -ऊ , the glide -य- does not occur (dialectally and in older Hindī the glide -व- may occur), but the stem-vowel is shortened: छुआ, छुए , छुई from the stem छू- .

§ 300. There are six verbs with irregular perfective participles:

जाना	to go	गया *	गये/गए	गयी/गई
लेना	to take	लिया	लिये/लिए	ली
देना	to give	दिया	दिये/दिए	दी
करना	to do	किया	किये/किए	की
होना	to be	हुआ	हुए	हुई
मरना	to die	मुआ **	मुए	मुई

* In certain combinations जाया.
** मुआ is archaic and/or dialectal. Standard Hindī uses the regular form मरा .

THE VERBAL SYSTEM.

§ 301. The verbal system in Hindi is formed in the following way: either Aspect-markers + Gender-Number or Person-Number markers are added to the STEM, with or without the auxiliary होना. We distinguish between three sub-systems: the INDICATIVE system, the SUBJUNCTIVE system, and the IMPERATIVE system, of which the first two include the auxiliary होना.

§ 302. THE AUXILIARY VERB होना "to be". *

As auxiliary होना occurs in present, imperfect and irreal in the indicative system, and in potential and presumptive in the subjunctive system.

* As a main verb होना has all aspects, moods and tenses of any other verb, cf. §§ 315-316.

§ 303. SIMPLE PRESENT INDICATIVE of होना "to be".

The PN-morphemes, slightly modified, are added to the shorter stem ह्- :

	Sing.			Pl.		
1st pers.	(मैं)	हूँ	(I) am	(हम)	हैं	(we) are
2nd pers.	(तू)	है	(you) are	(तुम)	हो	(you) are
3rd pers.	(वह)	है	(he, she, it) is	(वे,आप)	हैं	(they, you) are

§ 304. IMPERFECT INDICATIVE.

GN-morphemes are added to the stem थ् (not derived from होना):

	Sing.		Pl.	
Masc.	था	was, were	थे	were
Fem.	थी	was, were	थीं	were

Note: Fem. pl. is ALWAYS nasalized.

§ 305. IRREAL.

The irreal is identical to the imperfective participle.

	Sing.		Pl.	
Masc.	होता	would be	होते	would be
Fem.	होती	would be	होतीं	would be

§ 306. ASPECTLESS POTENTIAL.

The PN-markers, sometimes contracted, are added to the stem हो – :

	Sing.		Pl.	
1st pers.	होऊँ		हों**	
2nd pers.	हो*	be, may be	हो, होम्रो	be, may be
3rd pers.	हो*		हों**	

* Older form: होए or होवे .

** Older form: होएँ or होवें.

§ 307. ASPECTLESS PRESUMPTIVE.

The aspectless presumptive is formed by adding the GN-marked suffix –गा to the simple potential:

	Sing.			Pl.		
	Masc.	Fem.		Masc.	Fem.	
1st. pers.	हूँगा*	हूँगी*		होंगे	होंगी	
2nd pers.	होगा	होगी	shall be	होगे	होगी	shall be
3rd pers.	होगा	होगी		होंगे	होंगी	

* or होऊँगा, होऊँगी.

§ 308. TABLES OF THE VERBAL SYSTEM.

1. THE INDICATIVE SYSTEM.

	Imperfective-habitual	Progressive-continuous	Perfective
Present	चलता है	चल रहा है	चला है
Past	चलता था	चल रहा था	चला था चला
Irreal	चलता चलता होता	चल रहा होता	चला होता

2. THE SUBJUNCTIVE SYSTEM.

	Aspect-less	Imperfective-habitual	Progressive-continuous	Perfective
Potential	चले	चलता हो	चल रहा हो	चला हो
Presumptive	चलेगा	चलता होगा	चल रहा होगा	चला होगा

3. THE IMPERATIVE SYSTEM.

	Sing.	Plur.	Impersonal
2nd pers.	चल	चलो	चलना
3rd pers.	void	चलिए	चलिएगा

§ 309. THE IMPERFECTIVE-HABITUAL ASPECT.

The imperfective aspect indicates that the action is incomplete; it is often habitual and/or repeatedly performed. The two tenses of the imperfective-habitual aspect, i.e. present and past in the indicative system, are formed as follows: the stem takes the aspect-marker -त्- + GN-markers + simple present or imperfect indicative of the auxiliary होना .

§ 310. IMPERFECTIVE-HABITUAL PRESENT INDICATIVE

मैं	चलता / चलती	हूँ	I (masc. or fem.) (usually) go
तू	चलता / चलती	है	you (usually) go
वह	चलता / चलती	है	he, she, it (usually) goes
हम	चलते / चलती	हैं	we (usually) go
तुम	चलते / चलती	हो	you (usually) go
वे	चलते / चलती	हैं	they (usually) go
ग्राप	चलते / चलती	हैं	you (hon.) (usually) go

§ 311. The imperfective present indicative is used in the following ways:

1. expressing a fact:

शेर गोश्त खाता है. — A lion eats meat.

मैं बम्बई में रहता हूँ. — I live in Bombay.

2. an often repeated action:

मैं रोज़ बाज़ार जाता हूँ. — I go to the market every day.

3. an immediate future:

मैं बताती हूँ. — I'll tell [you].

इतने में मैं लड़के के पास बैठती हूँ. — Meanwhile I'll sit with the boy.

वह ग्रभी जाता है. — He's going right now.

4. in stage-directions:

ग्रम्मा चेतना को पत्र देती है. — The mother gives a letter to Cetnā.

चेतना पत्र खोलती है. — Cetnā opens the letter.

5. as a narrative past, often translated with "would" in English:

सबेरे वह कुसुम से पूछ लेती. She would ask Kusum next morning.

When the verb is used as a narrative tense, the auxiliary is often deleted.

§ 312. IMPERFECTIVE-HABITUAL PAST INDICATIVE

	Sing.	Plur.
Masc.	(मैं, तू, वह) चलता था (I, you, he, it) went, used to go	(हम,तुम,वे,आप) चलते थे (we, you, they, you) went, used to go
Fem.	(मैं, तू, वह) चलती थी (I, you, she, it) went, used to go	(हम,तुम,वे,आप) चलती थीं (we, you, they, you) went, used to go

Note that only GN-markers occur in imperfective past.

§ 313. The imperfective past indicative is used in the same way as the imperfective present, i.e. the aspect underlines the fact that the action is habitual:

शाम को औरतें रोटी बनाती थीं और झाड़ू देती थीं.
In the evening the women used to/would make *roṭis* and sweep.

वे बड़े मकान में रहते थे. They lived in a big house.

उस समय मैं आठवें दर्जे में पढ़ता था.
At that time I was studying in the 8th grade.

पाकिस्तान में हम उर्दू और पंजाबी बोलते थे.
In Pākistān we used to speak Urdū and Panjābī.

§ 314. The NEGATION used for the imperfective present and past indicative is usually नहीं, but न may also occur, particularly in the imperfective past. The auxiliary is normally deleted in the imperfective present and the nasal is then transferred to the participle in **fem. plur.** (but not in masc. plur.):

लड़कियाँ बाज़ार नहीं जातीं. The girls do not usually go to the market.

वे औरतें हिन्दी नहीं बोलतीं. Those women do not speak Hindī.

THE IMPERFECTIVE PRESENT AND PAST INDICATIVE OF होना

§ 315. As stated earlier (§ 302), होना as a **main** verb takes all the aspects in the same way as any other verb. However, there is a distinct difference in the use of simple present indicative of होना and imperfective present. While the simple present indicative है expresses an **individual** fact, होता है expresses a **universal** fact, i.e. something the speaker considers a generally known, universally accepted fact.

घास का रंग हरा होता है.	Grass is green.
वह घास सूखी है.	That grass is dry.
आदमी के दो कान होते हैं.	Man has two ears.
आदमी बाहर है.	The man is outside.
एक अकेली मछली से हज़ारों बच्चे होते हैं.	One single fish has thousands of issue.
आज मछली बहुत अच्छी है.	The fish is very good today.
बच्चे को पिता से ज़्यादा मां की ज़रूरत होती है.	A child needs its mother more than its father.
हम को दूध की ज़रूरत है.	We need milk.

§ 316. As with all other verbs the imperfective aspect expresses a habitual state:

शाम को हम घर पर होते हैं.	We are usually at home in the evening.
टाइप होता है.	Typing done (here).
घड़ियों की मरम्मत होती है.	Watches are repaired (here).
कर्नल साहब के घर में ऐसा होता था.	In Colonel Sāhab's house it was [always] like this.

THE PROGRESSIVE-CONTINUOUS ASPECT.

§ 317. The progressive-continuous aspect indicates that the action is ongoing at a particular moment, present or past. **It is never habitual.** The two tenses of the progressive-continuous aspect, i.e. present and past, are formed in the following way: short absolutive of the main verb (identical to the stem) + the progressive aspect-marker रह् + GN-markers + simple present or imperfect indicative of the auxiliary होना:

1. THE PROGRESSIVE PRESENT INDICATIVE:

मैं	चल रहा / रही	हूँ	I am going
तू	चल रहा / रही	है	You are going
वह	चल रहा / रही	है	He/she/it is going
हम	चल रहे / रही	हैं	We are going
तुम	चल रहे / रही	हो	You are going
वे,आप	चल रहे / रही	हैं	They, you are going

2. THE PROGRESSIVE PAST INDICATIVE:

	Sing.		Plur.	
Masc.	(मैं,तू,वह)	चल रहा था	(हम,तुम,वे,आप)	चल रहे थे
Fem.		चल रही थी		चल रही थीं
		was, were going		were going

§ 318. Examples of the use of the progressive present indicative are:

मोहन कहाँ है? वह सो रहा है.	Where is Mohan? He is sleeping.
लड़की किताब पढ़ रही है.	The girl is reading a book.
आदमी खेत पर काम कर रहा है.	The man is working in the field.

§ 319. The progressive present may also express an immediate future:

मैं कल आ रहा हूँ.	I am coming tomorrow.
वह अभी आ रही है.	She'll come right away.

§ 320. The progressive past indicative is used in the same way as the progressive present:

गोपाल सिगरेट पी रहा था.	Gopāl was smoking a cigarette.
सीता कलकत्ते जा रही थी.	Sītā was on her way to Calcuttā.
सर्द हवा तेज़ी से बह रही थी.	The cold wind was blowing violently.
हम चुपचाप सुन रहे थे.	We were listening in silence.
वह छत पर सो रही थी.	She was sleeping on the roof.

THE PERFECTIVE ASPECT.

§ 321. The perfective aspect signifies that the action is **completed**. It indicates a **singular** event in the past, not a habitual or progressive action. The perfective aspect is formed by using the perfective participle, i.e. the stem + zero marker + GN-markers. There are three ways of expressing the completed past: 1. THE SIMPLE PERFECTIVE, 2. THE PRESENT PERFECTIVE, and 3. THE PAST PERFECTIVE (see below for formation and use).

§ 322. AGREEMENT.

In tenses where the PERFECTIVE ASPECT occurs, the relationship between the subject and the verb of the sentence is treated differently depending on whether the verb is object-taking (**सकर्मक क्रिया**) or non-object-taking (**अकर्मक क्रिया**).
Accordingly, there are three different sentence **constructions** in Hindī: THE SUBJECTIVE CONSTRUCTION, THE OBJECTIVE CONSTRUCTION, and THE NEUTRAL CONSTRUCTION.

§ 323. THE SUBJECTIVE CONSTRUCTION means that the verb agrees in gender, number, and person with the subject of the sentence, which then is always in **direct case**. This construction is used with all aspects if the verb is non-object-taking, and with imperfective and progressive aspects only if the verb is object-taking:

भारत स्वतन्त्र हुआ.	India became independent.
वह साइकिल से उतरा.	He got off the bicycle.
वह देर से लौटी है.	She has returned late.
आदमी काम करता था.	The man worked.
लड़की बिल्ली देख रहा है.	The girl is looking at a cat.

§ 324. THE OBJECTIVE CONSTRUCTION is used with object-taking verbs in perfective tenses. The verb agrees in gender and number with the **direct object** of the sentence, provided the direct object is in **direct case** (see § 66). The **subject** of the sentence is always in **oblique case** followed by the postposition ने (see § 80):

ग्रौरत ने केला खाया.	The woman ate a banana.
मैं ने किताब पढ़ी है.	I have read the book.
उस ने बड़ा मकान देखा.	He saw a big house.
मोहन ने रास्ते पर साइकिल छोड़ी.	Mohan left the bicycle on the road.

§ 325. THE NEUTRAL CONSTRUCTION is a variant of the objective construction. It occurs when the direct object takes oblique case + को (see §§ 71, 81.1). The finite verb is always in **masc. sing. 3rd pers.** :

मैं ने ग्रौरत को देखा.	I saw the woman.
शेर ने सीता को खा लिया.	The tiger ate Sītā.
मच्छरों ने उसे काटा होगा.	The mosquitoes must have bitten him.

§ 326. A limited number of verbs that take a direct object in English are considered non-object-taking in Hindī, thus keeping the subjective construction in the perfective aspect. Such verbs are डरना "to fear", लड़ना "to fight", मिलना "to meet", बोलना "to speak", भूलना "to forget", समझना "to understand", and लाना "to bring".

§ 327. डरना, लड़ना, मिलना and बोलना are all constructed with the postposition से:

मैं विमला से मिला.	I met Vimlā.
बच्चा कुत्ते से डरता है.	The child is afraid of the dog.
वह मुझ से बोला.	He said to me.

The noun or pronoun that may precede the postposition is not to be interpreted as a direct object. It is the **indirect** object. Cf. §§ 83.2, 475.

§ 328. If there is a direct object in the sentence, बोलना, भूलना, and समझना usually become object-taking verbs:
मैं बोला "I said", but मोहन ने झूट बोला "Mohan lied" (lit. Mohan told a lie). However, to avoid ambiguity, भूलना and समझना as non-object-taking verbs are often combined with जाना **1** (see § 420):
मैं भूल गया "I forgot", but मैं ने किताब भूली, वह समझ गया "he understood", but उस ने कुछ नहीं समझा "he did not understand anything".
लाना is a contraction of ले ग्राना, lit. "to come having brought X, to come with X".

PERFECTIVE TENSES.

§ 329. THE SIMPLE PERFECTIVE indicates that the GN-marked perfective participle itself is used as a finite verb without any auxiliary (see §§ 298-300):

	Sing.		Plur.			
Masc.	चला	देखा	चले	देखे		
Fem.	चली	देखी	चलीं	देखीं	went	saw

It is used for a past event without any particular relation to the present time. It indicates that the action is single, completed and not habitual:

लड़का चला गया.	The boy went away.
रास्ते पर मुझे एक दोस्त मिला.	On the road I ran into a friend.
मैं ने चाय पी ली.	I drank tea.
राम ने जंगल में बड़ा शेर देखा.	Rām saw a big tiger in the jungle.
राम ने दो चिट्ठियाँ लिखीं.	Rām wrote two letters.
किसी ने दरवाज़ा खोला.	Somebody opened the door.

§ 330. In conditional sentences, the simple perfective is used when the second action depends on the completion of the first:

अगर मैं बीमार पड़ गया तो डाकटर के पास जाऊँगा.
If I fall ill, I shall go to a doctor.

§ 331. The simple perfective is used idiomatically to indicate an immediate future:

आप चलिए, मैं अभी आया.	You please go, I'll come right away.
बचाओ, बचाओ, मर गया.	Help! Help! I am dying!

§ 332. THE PRESENT PERFECTIVE is formed with the GN-marked perfective participle + the simple present indicative of the auxiliary होना:

मैं	चला/चली हूँ	I have gone
तू	चला/चली है	you have gone
वह	चला/चली है	he (she) has gone
हम	चले/चली हैं	we have gone
तुम	चले/चली हो	you have gone
वे, आप	चले/चली हैं	they, you have gone

§ 333. The present perfective indicates that even though the action is completed its result extends into the present time:

वह आया है.	He has come (i.e. he is here).
किस ने ये फूल तोड़े हैं?	Who has picked these flowers?
मै आप का नाश्ता लाया हूँ.	I have brought your breakfast.

§ 334. If the present perfective is negated, the auxiliary can be deleted:

वह नहीं गया.	He has not gone (i.e. he is still here).
मैं ने गीता नहीं पढ़ी.	I have not read the Bhagavadgītā.

In fem. plur. the nasal is carried over to the perfective participle:

लड़कियाँ नहीं आईं.	The girls have not come.

Note that the negated present perfective coincides with the simple perfective.

§ 335. Certain verbs such as बैठना "to sit down", लेटना "to lie down", and पड़ना "to fall" are dynamic in Hindī: the perfective participle "having sat down" implies that the action is **completed** and, consequently, the person **is sitting**. Hence these verbs are usually translated with progressive present or past in English:

मैं बिस्तर पर लेटा हूँ.	I am lying on the bed.
किताब मेज़ पर पड़ी है.	The book is lying on the table.
वह बाहर बैठा था.	He was sitting outside.

§ 336. THE PAST PERFECTIVE is formed with the GN-marked perfective participle + simple past indicative of the auxiliary होना:

	Sing.	Plur.	
Masc.	चला था	चले थे	
Fem.	चली थी	चली थीं	had gone

§ 337. The past perfective is used for a more remote past. It often indicates that one action is completed before another action in the past:

उस ने अपनी बुआ को चिट्ठी लिखी थी.
He had written a letter to his aunt.

वह सो गई थी. — She had fallen asleep.

तारा ने वही बात कही जो केशव ने कही थी.
Tārā said precisely what Keśav had said.

सब बच्चे बाहर निकल गए क्योंकि बारिश बन्द हो गई थी.
All the children went out because the rain had stopped.

THE CONTRARY-TO-FACT or THE IRREAL.

§ 338. The IRREAL describes the action as contrary-to-fact. For example: Had he been there, this would not have happened. However, a contrary-to-fact statement is also a factual statement as it makes a claim about the world. It is logical, therefore, to classify the irreal as belonging to the indicative system, even though it may often be rendered by a subjunctive when translated into English.

§ 339. THE IRREAL exists in all three aspects: 1. imperfective irreal, 2. progressive irreal, and 3. perfective irreal. The IMPERFECTIVE IRREAL is of two kinds:

1. (a) identical with the imperfective participle (चलता, देखता)
   (b) the imperfective participle of the main verb + the imperfective participle of होना,

2. the PROGRESSIVE IRREAL is formed with the stem + the progressive aspect-marker रह् + GN-marker + the imperfective participle of होना,

3. the PERFECTIVE IRREAL is formed with the perfective participle of the main verb + the imperfective participle of होना.

		Sing.	Plur.
Imperfective aspect:	Masc.	चलता	चलते
		चलता होता	चलते होते
	Fem.	चलती	चलतीं
		चलती होती	चलती होतीं
		would go	
		would usually go	
Progressive aspect:	Masc.	चल रहा होता	चल रहे होते
	Fem.	चल रही होती	चल रही होतीं
		would be going	

Perfective aspect:	Masc.	चला होता	चले होते
	Fem.	चली होती	चली होतीं
		would have gone	

§ 340. Irreal forms are used in conditional clauses, where it is taken for granted that the condition is not fulfilled or impossible to fulfill. The usage is illustrated by the following examples:

अगर डिब्बे में और सवारियाँ होतीं तो शायद मैं छिप जाता.
Had there been other passengers in the compartment, I could perhaps have hidden.

मैं थाने न जाता तो शायद कभी घर न पहुँच पाता.
Had I not gone to the police-station, perhaps I could never have reached home.

अगर मैं और बड़ा व मज़बूत होता तो मैं ख़ुद ही उसे मार डालता.
If I were bigger and stronger I would kill him myself.

अगर वह यह तमाशा न देखता होता.
If he did not [always] see this spectacle!

यदि बारिश न हो रही होती तो हम बाहर निकलते.
If it were not raining, we would go out.

मैं चाहता हूँ कि उस चिट्ठी को न लिखा होता.
I wish I had not written that letter.

अगर वह न आया होता तो उन्हों ने मुझे मार ही डाला होता.
If he had not come, they would have killed me.

Note also:

मैं चुप रही. क्या कहती. — I remained silent. What could I say?
तू आई क्यों? वहीं रह जाती. — Why did you come? You should have stayed there.

THE SUBJUNCTIVE SYSTEM.

§ 341. While the indicative mood expresses an objective, factual statement, the subjunctive mood expresses a subjective evaluation of the action as something the speaker wants, wishes, would want or wish, supposes, presumes, considers possible, fears or doubts.

The subjunctive mood comprises 1. POTENTIALS, and 2. PRESUMPTIVES.

1. The POTENTIAL denotes a possibility: the action may or may not occur. For example: I think he may come.

2. The PRESUMPTIVE expresses a greater certainty: the speaker presumes the action will occur. For example: I think he will come. The grammatical category "future" belongs here: "future" in Hindī is a mood, not a tense. Morphologically the so-called "future" is an integral part of the subjunctive system. We have chosen to call the "future" presumptive, because it is logically impossible to make a factual statement about what has not yet happened.

§ 342. The subjunctive system comprises the same three aspects as the indicative system: imperfective-habitual, progressive-continuous, and perfective. In addition, the subjunctive system has two ASPECTLESS paradigms.

Tenses in the subjunctive system depend on aspect and context.

TABLE.

	Aspectless	Imperfective	Progressive	Perfective
Potential	चले	चलता हो	चल रहा हो	चला हो
Presumptive	चलेगा	चलता होगा	चल रहा होगा	चला होगा

§ 343. The ASPECTLESS POTENTIAL is formed by adding the PN-markers directly to the verbal stem:

मैं	चलूँ	I may go	हम	चलें	we may go
तू	चले	you may go	तुम	चलो	you may go
वह	चले	he/she/it may go	वे/आप	चलें	they/you may go

§ 344. Stems in -ई and -ऊ shorten the stem-vowel before PN-markers, पिऊँ "I may drink" from पीना, etc. (cf. § 299.2,3, also §§ 35, 37). The verbs लेना and देना have special, contracted forms:

मैं दूँ/लूँ	I may give/take	हम	दें/लें	we may give/take
तू दे/ले	you may give	तम	दो/लो	you may give/take
वह दे/ले	he/she may give/take	वे,आप	दें/लें	they/you may give/take

§ 345. The aspectless potential expresses a wish, a hope, a suggestion, a supposition, a polite request, an exhortation, or a polite command:

तो फिर ऐसा ही हो. May it be so then!
आप को भगवान शान्ति दे. May God give you peace!
मैं चाहता हूँ कि आप की उम्र लम्बी हो.
I wish you a long life.
शायद इसी दुकान में आटा मिले. Maybe one can get flour in this shop.
मम्मी, क्या हम आइसक्रीम लें? Mummy, can we have ice cream?
मैं तुम्हारे पास आई हूँ कि तुम भी मुझ से प्रेम करो.
I have come to you so that you also may love me.

§ 346. The IMPERFECTIVE POTENTIAL is formed with the imperfective participle + the simple potential of the auxiliary होना :

मैं चलता/ती होऊँ	I may go, etc.	हम चलते/ती हों
तू चलता/ती हो		तुम चलते/ती होओ/हो
वह चलता/ती हो		वे,आप चलते/ती हों

The imperfective potential underlines that the action is habitual:
शायद वह पुरानी दिल्ली में रहती हो. Perhaps she lives in Old Delhi.
शायद वह यहाँ काम करता हो. Perhaps he works here.

§ 347. The PROGRESSIVE POTENTIAL is formed as the progressive present indicative, but with the aspectless potential form of the auxiliary होना:
मैं चल रहा/रही होऊँ etc.
The progressive potential underlines the fact that the action is going on at the moment:
वह किसी होटल में रह रहा हो. He may be staying in some hotel.
शायद वह पढ़ रहा हो. Maybe he is studying.

§ 348. The PERFECTIVE POTENTIAL is formed with the GN-marked perfective participle + the aspectless potential of होना :

मैं चला/चली होऊँ etc.

The perfective potential indicates that the action, that may have taken place, is completed:

यदि उस ने झूठ बोला हो तो उसे निकाल दो.
If he has lied throw him out!

ऐसा शोर हुआ जैसे बिजली गिरी हो.
There was a noise as if lightning had struck.

वह आ गया हो. — He may have come.

सम्भव है कि पास वाली पान की दुकान पर आया हो.
It is possible that he may have gone to the nearby betel-stall.

उन्हों ने उसे लखनाऊ में देखा हो. — They may have seen him in Lucknow.

§ 349. Potential forms are used after जैसे and मानो "as if":

ऐसा लगता है मानो फूलों की प्रदर्शनी लग रही हो.
It appears as if a flower exhibition is going on.

मानो सारा कश्मीर ही एक बहुत बड़ा बाग हो.
...as if the whole of Kashmir were one very big garden.

मानो वह कोई खिलौना हो, कोई पक्षी हो जो लाया गया हो.
...as if she were a toy, a bird which had been brought [here].

जैसे किसी विषैले बिच्छू ने उसे काट खाया हो.
... as if a poisonous scorpion had bitten her.

ऐसा लग रहा था मानो हम किसी और ही दुनिया में आ पहुंचे हों.
It seemed as if we had arrived in an entirely different world.

§ 350. The ASPECTLESS PRESUMPTIVE is formed by adding the GN-marked suffix -गा to the aspectless potential:

मैं	चलूँगा/गी	I shall go, etc.	हम	चलेंगे/गी
तू	चलेगा/गी		तुम	चलोगे/गी
वह	चलेगा/गी		वे,आप	चलेंगे/गी

§ 351. The aspectless presumptive implies that the speaker assumes with a certain degree of certainty that an action must happen. Since all utterances regarding the future are bound to be presumptive, one of the functions of the aspectless presumptive is to express the FUTURE TENSE in Hindī.

दिल्ली में बिजली के रेट बढ़ेंगे. — The electricity rates in Delhi will rise.
मैं कल यह किताब पढ़ूँगा. — I'll read this book tomorrow.
सन २००० में भारत की आबादी १०० करोड़ हो जाएगी. — In the year 2000 India's population will be 100 crores (i.e. 1 billion).
क्या कुछ और खाओगे? — Will you eat something else?

But note expressions such as
यह कहना गलत होगा कि ... — It would be wrong to say that ...
मैं आप से पूछना चाहूँगा कि... — I would like to ask you ...
मैं आप से क्या चाहूँगा? — What would I want from you?

§ 352. The aspectless presumptive is negated with either न or नहीं:

मैं भी नहीं खाऊँगा. — I will not eat either.
क्या तुम कपड़े न बदलोगी? — Are you not going to change clothes?

§ 353. The IMPERFECTIVE PRESUMPTIVE is formed with the GN-marked imperfective participle + aspectless presumptive of the auxiliary होना:

मैं चलता/ती हूँगा/गी etc.

The imperfective presumptive indicates that the speaker presumes that the action is habitual and imperfective:

वह किसी गाँव में रहता होगा. — He (presumably, surely) lives in a village.
आप जानते होंगे. — You surely know.
आप को यहाँ डर तो लगता होगा. — You must be scared here.

§ 354. The PROGRESSIVE PRESUMPTIVE is formed with the short absolutive + the GN-marked progressive aspect-marker रहा + aspectless presumptive of होना:

मैं चल रहा/ी हूँगा/गी etc.

The progressive presumptive implies that the speaker presumes the action is going on at the moment:

बाज़ारों में नदी बह रही होगी.	The river must be rising in the bazaars.
ग्राप को देर हो रही होगी.	You will (surely) be getting late.
मोहन घबरा रहा होगा.	Mohan must be worrying.

§ 355. The PERFECTIVE PRESUMPTIVE is formed with the GN-marked perfective participle + aspectless presumptive of होना:

मैं चला/ी हूँगा/गी etc.

Note that object-taking verbs in perfective presumptive take either the objective or the neutral construction (§§ 324-325).

वह चला गया होगा.	He must have gone away.
किसी ने उसे लिया होगा.	Somebody must have taken it.
तुम ने गान्धीजी की ग्रात्मकथा ज़रूर पढ़ी होगी.	Surely you must have read Gandhī's autobiography.
ज़रूर कोई जानवर कुएँ में गिर कर मर गया होगा.	Surely some animal must have fallen into the well and died [there].

THE IMPERATIVE SYSTEM.

§ 356. The imperative exists in the following forms:

1. (तू) चल, देख	PN-marker: Ø
2. (तुम) चलो, देखो	PN-marker: -ग्रो
3. (ग्राप) चलिए, देखिए	PN-marker: -इए (also spelt -इये)
4. चलना, देखना	neutral and invariable
5. चलिएगा, देखिएगा	neutral and invariable

§ 357. Imperatives of the type चल "go!", देख "look!" are identical with the verbal stem. This imperative is used when the pronoun of address is तू (see §132). Consequently, it is used in the same way as तू, that is:

1. in intimate, affectionate speech between mother and child, between lovers in private, in poetry and in prayers:

काकी ने उसे गोद में लिया - न रो, राजा.
His aunt took him in her lap: "Don't weep, darling!"

बेट्टे, मूंह-हाथ धो!	Son, go and have a wash ! (Lit. wash [your] face and hands!)
हे भगवान, हमारी मदद कर!	O God, help us!

2. to express anger, contempt or disgust. It is used to address children, servants or any person who does not command respect, and to animals:

चुप रह!	Shut up!
डूब मर, साले!	Go drown yourself, [you] bastard!
मुए कत्ते, हट!	Go away, [you] bloody dog!

§ 358. The imperative carrying the PN-marker -ओ (identical to the 2nd pers. plur. aspectless potential) is used when the pronoun of address is तुम (see §135). The verbs लेना and देना have the contracted forms लो and दो (cf. § 344).

The imperative in -ओ follows the same rules for usage as तुम, i.e. it is used between friends and social equals, to family members of the same age or younger, and in all informal relationships. It is also used for people whom the speaker considers socially inferior. It is the normal imperative used to servants and workmen of all kinds. It is also the normal polite imperative in villages where the local dialect does not have the formal pronoun of address आप.

आओ, चलो!	Come, let's go!
यह काम जल्दी करो!	Do this work quickly!
बैरा, एक प्याला चाय लाओ!	Waiter, bring [me] a cup of tea!
सीढ़ियों के सामने गाड़ी रोक दो!	Stop the car in front of the steps!

§ 359. The imperative carrying the PN-marker -इए/-इये is used for every formal occasion, when the pronoun of address is आप (see § 137). It has a wide usage, because Indian society is more formal than North American society. The ending as such carries the value implied in English "please".

Irregular formal imperatives are: लीजिए from लेना "to take", दीजिए from देना "to give", पीजिए from पीना "to drink", and कीजिए from करना "to do".

> Note: there is a regularly formed formal imperative करिए from करना. This form, however, is familiar and/or dialectal.

आइए. बैठिए!	Please come [in]! Sit down!
यह किताब पढ़िए!	Please read this book!
मेरी मदद कीजिए!	Please help me!
हमारी पार्टी में शामिल होइये!	Please join our party!

§ 360. The imperative of the type चलना, देखना is identical with the infinitive, but, as an imperative, it is always INVARIABLE. This imperative is considered neutral with regards to pronouns of address. However, from actual usage it seems that this imperative is more closely connected with the pronoun तुम. It is also used for general rules and prescriptions. This imperative is sometimes called "future imperative". There is, however, nothing in the actual usage that makes this imperative more "future" than any other imperative:

वेटर, चाय लाना.	Waiter, bring tea!
बेटे, अभी दूध पीना.	Son, drink [your] milk right now!
मुझ से न डरना.	Don't be afraid of me!
बेटे, तुम शराब कभी मत पीना.	Son, don't ever drink liquor!
ज़मीन पर मत थूकना.	Don't spit on the floor!

§ 361. The imperative in -इएगा is the most formal. It is supposed to be neutral as far as pronouns of address are concerned. However, if a pronoun is indicated – and it sometimes is – it is always आप. This imperative is often called "future imperative" because it has the suffix -गा. Actual usage shows that the time-aspect in both -इएगा and -इए is basically the same. Note that the suffix -गा in this form is INVARIABLE.

उन से पूछिएगा.	Please ask him/them!
एक बात आप याद रखिएगा.	Please keep one thing in mind!
देर मत कीजिएगा.	Please don't delay!
मुझे ये किताबें भिजवा दीजिएगा.	Please have these books sent to me!

CAUSATIVE VERBS.

§ 362. Causative verbs (प्रेरणार्थक क्रिया) describe an action which is initiated by one person, the subject, but performed by another, the agent: "to have or to get something done [by someone else]." Causative verbs can only be created from object-taking verb (सकर्मक क्रिया).

§ 363. Causative verbs are normally marked by the morpheme -वा- added to the stem. Long stem-vowels are shortened, since the accent falls on the long vowel of the morpheme:

छापना	"to print"	छपवाना	"to have/get [something] printed"
काटना	"to cut"	कटवाना	"to have [something] cut"
पीटना	"to beat"	पिटवाना	"to have [somebody] beaten"
सीना	"to sew"	सिलवाना	"to have [something] sewn"
लूटना	"to loot"	लुटवाना	"to have [something] looted"
बेचना	"to sell"	बिकवाना	"to have [something] sold"
खोलना	"to open"	खुलवाना	"to have [something] opened"
जलाना	"to burn"	जलवाना	"to have [something] burned"

§ 364. There are also causative verbs in -आना, often with a parallel form in -वाना :

करना	"to do"	कराना	
		करवाना	"to get [something] done"
लादना	"to load"	लदाना	
		लदवाना	"to get [something] loaded"
खोलना	"to open"	खुलाना	
		खुलवाना	"to have [something] opened"
छोड़ना	"to release"	छुढ़ाना	
		छुढ़वाना	"to have [somebody] released"
धोना	"to wash"	धुलाना	
		धुलवाना	"to have [something] washed"

Note that this list is not exhaustive.

§ 365. The agent in a causative sentence is often left unexpressed:

उसे ने अपने शत्रु का मकान जलवा दिया.
He had his enemy's house burnt down.

यह पत्र भिजवा देना. Have this letter sent!

उस ने गाड़ी लदवा दी. He had the car loaded.

§ 366. The agent, when expressed, takes the postposition से, or more formally (के) द्वारा/के ज़रिये (see §§ 94, 372):

मैं धोबी से कपड़े धुलाऊँगा. I'll get the clothes washed by the washerman.

नौकरों से कमरा साफ़ करवा देना.
Have the room cleaned by the servants!

किसान ने मज़दूरों से बैलगाड़ी सब्ज़ी से लदवा दी.
The farmer had his oxcart loaded with vegetables by the workers.

ज़मीनदार ने अपने गुण्डों से हरिजनों के झोंपड़े जलवा दिए.
The landlord had his hoodlums burn down the untouchables' huts.

§ 367. Compare the following sentences:

वहे खानो खाती है. She eats.

वहे बच्चे को खानो खिलाती है. She feeds the child.

वहे बच्चे को आयो से खानो खिलवाती है.
She gets the child fed by the nanny.

मैं हिन्दी पढ़ती हूँ. I study Hindī.

मैं अपने बेटे को हिन्दी पढ़ाती हूँ. I teach my son Hindī.

मैं अपने बेटे को अच्छे अध्यापके से हिन्दी पढ़वाती हूँ.
I have my son taught Hindī by a good teacher.

PASSIVE VOICE.

§ 368. The passive is formed by adding जाना to the GN-marked perfective participle. Both object-taking and non-object-taking verbs can be made passive. All tenses, aspects and moods – with the possible exception of the imperative – can be changed into the passive voice.

§ 369. TABLES. मारा जाना to be beaten

1. THE INDICATIVE SYSTEM.

	Habitual	Continuous
PRESENT	वह मारा जाता है	वह मारा जा रहा है
PAST	वह मारा जाता था	वह मारा जा रहा था
PAST	Perfective	
	वह मारा गया है	
	वह मारा गया था	
	वह मारा गया	
IRREAL	Habitual	Continuous
	वह मारा जाता	वह मारा जा रहा होता
	वह मारा जाता होता	
	Perfective	
	वह मारा गया होता	

2. THE SUBJUNCTIVE SYSTEM.

POTENTIAL	Aspectless	Habitual
	वह मारा जाए	वह मारा जाता हो
	Continuous	Perfective
	वह मारा जा रहा हो	वह मारा गया हो
PRESUMPTIVE	Aspectless	Habitual
	वह मारा जाएगा	वह मारा जाता होगा
	Continuous	Perfective
	वह मारा जा रहा होगा	वह मारा गया होगा

§ 370. Examples of the use of the passive:

चिट्ठी डाक से भेजी गई थी. The letter had been sent by mail.

दक्षिण भारत में हिन्दी नहीं बोली जाती.
Hindī is not spoken in South India.

दो घण्टे की बहस के बाद यह घोषणा की गई.
This announcement was made after two hours of discussion.

इस फ़िसाद में तो बेचारे ईसाई और पारसी भी मारे गए.
In this trouble poor Christians and Pārsīs were killed too.

§ 371. As a main verb in the passive voice the verb जाना has the perfective participle जाया:

तो क्या तुम चाहती हो कि इस का निर्णय करने के लिए अदालत में जाया जाए.
Do you then wish that we go to court to decide about this?

§ 372. As noted in the above examples, the agent is often not expressed. If there is a precise agent in a passive sentence, it takes the oblique case + the postpositions से or, more formally, के द्वारा/द्वारा, के ज़रिये (see § 94):

राम मोहन से मारा गया. Rām was killed by Mohan.
प्रधान मन्त्री के द्वारा निश्चय किया गया है.
The decision has been taken by the Prime Minister.

§ 373. Normally, the subject and object in the active sentence become the agent and the subject in the passive sentence. Hindī, however, also has the option of maintaining the object in the active sentence as the object in the passive sentence. The finite passive verb is then always in the **3rd person masc. sing.** This is called IMPERSONAL PASSIVE:

जीप में श्रीमती गान्धी को बिठाया गया.
Mrs Gāndhī was seated in the jeep. (Lit. It was seated regarding Mrs. Gāndhī ...)

उसे बताया गया था कि अशोक वापस आ गया.
She had been told that Aśok had come back.
(Lit. It had been told to her...)

शरणार्थियों को भिन्न भिन्न कैम्पों में भेजा जा रहा था.
The refugees were being sent to different camps.

गहनों को कहाँ बेचा जाए? Where can the jewellery be sold?

§ 374. In a negated or interrogative clause the passive voice may express inability or ability to perform the action. The impersonal passive is normally used in this type of sentences:

मुझ से सोया नहीं गया. I could not sleep.
राम से काम नहीं किया जाता. Rām can't work.
मुझ से अभी बाज़ार नहीं जाया जाएगा. I will not be able to go to the bazaar right now.
उस से बिना बोले न रहा गया. He could not refrain from speaking.
लालबिहारी से यह सहा न गया. Lālbihārī could not endure this.
रात भर वह यही सोचता रहा कि उस देश में कैसे पहुँचा जाए. All night he kept thinking: "How can I reach that country?"

§ 375. Combined verbs can be made passive:

सुधा का सब सामान कमरे में रख दिया गया. All Sudhā's luggage was put in the room.
हिन्दी बहुत लोगों से राष्ट्रभाषा के रूप में स्वीकार कर ली गई थी. Hindī had been accepted by many people as the national language.

§ 376. Causative verbs can be made passive. It is, however, virtually impossible to translate this into an English passive:

यह बाग शाह जहाँ से लगवाया गया. Shah Jahān had this garden planted.
मेरे पिताजी से मन्दिर बनवाया गया. My father had the temple built.

PARTICIPLES.

§ 377. The two most important participles in Hindi are the imperfective and the perfective participles.There is also the less frequently used progressive participle. These participles are used to form finite verbs as illustrated by the verbal system. Finally, there are also a passive and a completive participle (see §§ 386-387).

§ 378. As infinite verbal forms the participles function as GN-marked ADJECTIVES. Consequently, they take the same endings as GN-marked adjectives (see § 203), and they take both direct and oblique case:

	Imperfective	Progressive	Perfective
Masc. sg. dir.	देखता	देख रहा	देखा
Masc. sg. obl.	देखते	देख रहे	देखे
Masc. pl. dir. and obl.	देखते	देख रहे	देखे
Fem. sg. and pl. dir. and obl.	देखती	देख रही	देखी

§ 379. The imperfective participle is active; the progressive participle is active if the verb is object-taking and passive if the verb is non-object-taking; the perfective participle is always passive. As adjectives, the imperfective and the perfective participles may be followed by the GN-marked perfective participle of the auxiliary होना, i.e. हुआ. This added हुआ does not serve any other purpose than to indicate that the preceding participle is used as an adjective: consequently, it should not be translated. This use of the participle as an adjective often corresponds to a relative clause in English:

चलती (हुई) गाड़ी	a running train
रोता (हुआ) लड़का	a weeping boy
खेलते (हुए) बच्चे	playing children
उड़ती (हुई) चिड़ियाँ	flying birds
बन रही सड़क	a road [that is] being built
किताब पढ़ रहा लड़का	a boy [who is] reading a book
लिखा (हुआ) पत्र	a written letter
भेजी (हुई) पार्सल	a parcel [that] has been sent
पिये (हुए) आदमी	drunk men
मारी (हुई) औरतें	beaten women

§ 380. Like adjectives, imperfective, progressive and perfective participles can be used attributively, but only the perfective can be used predicatively. The imperfective and the progressive participles cannot be used predicatively since that would amount to a finite verb in imperfective and progressive aspect respectively. Thus:

बहता पानी साफ़ होता है.	Running water is clean.
बाग में खिलते हुए फूल तोड़ रही है.	She is picking blooming flowers in the garden.
इस से मैं यह बड़ी जल्दी में लिखा पत्र बस करता हूँ.	With this I finish this very hastily written letter.
मकान पिछले साल बनाये हुए थे.	The houses were built last year.

§ 381. Like other adjectives, the imperfective and perfective participles can become nouns, and are then declined like nouns:
डूबता masc. a drowning [man], मरी fem. a dead [woman]

	Masc.	Fem.	Masc.	Fem.
Sing. dir.	डूबता	डूबती	मरा	मरी
Sing. obl.	डूबते	डूबती	मरे	मरी
Plur. dir.	डूबते	डूबतियाँ	मरे	मरियाँ
Plur. obl.	डूबतों	डूबतियों	मरों	मरियों

उस ने रोतों को चावल दिया.	He gave rice to the weeping.
डूबते को बचाओ.	Save the drowning [man]!
पढ़े-लिखों को नौकरी ज़रूर मिलेगी.	The educated will certainly get jobs.
उस ने मरी को ज़मीन पर रखा.	He put the dead [woman] on the ground.

ADVERBIAL PARTICIPLES.

§ 382. The imperfective and the perfective participles can both be used adverbially. The imperfective participle indicates that the action is simultaneous with the main action as expressed in the finite verb, the perfective participle indicates an action preceding the main action.
Used adverbially the participle is treated in one of the following three ways (cf. § 238) :

1. as masc. sing. oblique in -ए regardless of the gender and number of the main word:

उस ने लड़की को गाते सुना.	He heard the girl singing.
मैं ने मोहन को आते हुए देखा.	I saw Mohan coming.

उसे गए दो महीने हो गए.	Two months have passed since he left.
बैठे समय कुर्सी की पेठी बांधे रखिए.	Keep the seatbelt fastened while seated.

For बैठा see § 335.

2. GN-marked in agreement with the main word:

लड़की गीत गुनगुनाती हुई कमरे में आई.	The girl entered the room humming a song.
वह इन सब(ों)को छोड़ता हुआ आगे बढ़ने लगा.	Leaving them all [behind] he began to go forward.
उस ने खिड़की खुली छोड़ दी.	He left the window open.

3. as invariable masc. sing. in –आ :

आप को आता देखकर वह अपने किले में घुस गया है.	Having seen you coming he has gone into his fortress.
तुम सब लोग मुझे मरा हुआ क्यों नहीं मान लेते हो?	Why don't all of you presume me dead? (said by a woman)
उन्हों ने अपनी माँ, पत्नी और बेटे, सभी को वहाँ बैठा पाया.	He found his mother, wife and son all sitting there.

§ 383. The participle can be doubled for emphasis:

काम करते करते वह थक गया.	Working hard he got tired.
उस ने चलते चलते मुझ से कहा ...	While we were walking along he said to me…
वह पढ़ते पढ़ते सो गई.	She fell asleep while reading.

SPECIAL USES OF PARTICIPLES.

§ 384. Invariable masc. oblique imperfective participle + ही equals English "as soon as". The tense in translation will depend on the tense of the finite verb:

उसे देखते ही वह रोने लगी. — As soon as she saw him she began to weep.

उस के आते ही चोर भागा. — As soon as he came the thief fled.

पाँच बजते ही दफ़्तर बन्द हो जाता है. — As soon as it strikes five the office closes.

§ 385. The invariable masc. oblique perfective participle + बिना means "without V". बिना can precede the participle, or be placed after (cf. § 98):

बिना मुझे देखे वह चाय पीती रही. — Without having looked at me she kept on drinking tea.

बिना किसी से कुछ कहे हुए वह चला गया. — Without having said anything to anybody he went away.

उस से बिना बोले न रहा गया. — He couldn't refrain from talking.

§ 386. A completive participle can be formed by using the short absolutive + the GN-marked perfective participle of चुकना (see under चुकना § 420). It can only be used attributively:

प्रकाशित हो चुकी किताबें — books [already] published

कर चुका काम — work [already] done

तमिल मुक्ति चीतों ने एक मसज़िद में घुसकर नमाज़ अदा कर चुके पाँच मुसलमानों की हत्या कर दी. — The Tamil Liberation Tigers entered a mosque and killed five Muslims who had finished offering [their] prayers.

§ 387. Every object-taking verb can form a passive participle: लिखा गया "written", देखा गया "seen". However, it is seldom used, since the perfective participle of object-taking verbs already is passive in itself (see § 379).

THE INFINITIVE.

§ 388. The infinitive is formed by adding the infinitive-marker -ना to the verbal stem. This is the lexical form of a Hindī verb. (See § 294.) The infinitive is 1. an action noun, 2. an infinite verbal form, and 3. a verbal adjective.

§ 389. As an ACTION NOUN the infinitive is treated as a masc. noun in -आ:

Dir. case	खाना eating, the action of eating	चलना going
Obl. case	खाने	चलने

As an action noun the infinitive exists only in the SINGULAR, with the one exception of the idiomatic expression लेने के देने पड़ना "to be in danger, to have the tables turned":

अगर यहाँ से न भाग जाओगे तो लेने के देने पड़ेंगे.
If you don't run away from here you will be in danger.

§ 390. Like any other noun the infinitive can have modifiers:

राम का सुनना	Rām's hearing
मेरा आना	my coming
उस का मीठा बोलना	his sweet talk(ing)

§ 391. The infinitive as an action noun functions both as subject and object:

अन्दर आना मना है.	It is forbidden to enter.
मोहन का दौड़ना व्यर्थ है.	Mohan's running is useless.
उस का आना ज़रूरी है.	It is necessary that he comes.
झूठ बोलना बुरा है.	It is bad to tell lies.
चाचा के साथ रहना वीना को भाता नहीं.	Vīnā does not like to live with her uncle.
वह लिखना सीख रहा है.	He is learning to write.

§ 392. As a verbal form the infinitive can take any complements that a finite verb may take, such as adverbs and direct objects:

इधर जाना	to go there
भीख माँगना	to ask for alms
मैं किताबें लाना भूल गई.	I forgot to bring the books.

Note that in the last example लाना is the dir. obj. of the finite verb भूल गई, whereas किताबें is the dir. obj. of the infinitive लाना (see SYNTAX § 482).

THE OBLIQUE INFINITIVE + POSTPOSITION.

§ 393. The oblique infinitive + postposition is used in various ways constituting different kinds of adverbial clauses. These adverbial clauses often correspond to subordinate clauses in English.

§ 394. The oblique infinitive + को or के लिए expresses intention:

बच्चा रोज़ खेलने के लिए बाग़ जाता है.
The child goes daily to the garden to play.

माली ज़मीन खोदने के लिए नया फावड़ा ला रहा है.
The gardener is bringing a new shovel to dig the earth.

राम मुझ से मिलने को आया. — Rām came to meet me.

1. The postposition can be deleted, especially if the finite verb is a verb of motion:

मैं हिन्दी सीखने भारत आया था. — I had come to India to learn Hindī.
वह खाना खाने बैठ गया. — He sat down to eat.

2. The oblique infinitive + को + होना indicates that the action is imminent:

वह जाने को था. — He was about to go.
बच्चा डूबने ही को था कि नाविक ने उसे बचा लिया.
The child was just about to drown when the boatman saved him.

§ 395. The oblique infinitive + पर + होना indicates either

1. that the action is imminent:

रेलगाड़ी आने पर है. — The train is about to come.

2. or that it substitutes for a temporal clause:

घएटी की आवाज़ सुनने पर वह जगा.
When he heard the clock he woke up. (lit. Upon hearing the clock…)

दफ़तर वापस आने पर उस ने वहाँ किसी को न देखा.
When he returned to the office he did not see anybody there.

हमारे जाने पर उन्हों ने अपने रुपये गिने.
When we had gone they counted their money.

§ 396. The oblique infinitive + के बाद indicates an action which precedes the main action:

मन्दिर से निकलने के बाद मैं ने अपने जूते फिर पहन लिये.
After I had come out from the temple I put on my shoes again.

गाड़ी के छूटने के बाद मोहन आया. Mohan came after the train had left.

§ 397. The oblique infinitive + से is used in adverbial phrases:

ऐसा करने से आप सफल होंगे. You'll be successful by doing so.

दूध और बछड़े बेचने से किसान पैसे कमाता है.
The peasant earns money by selling milk and calves.

कुत्तों के भौंकने से हाथी नहीं डरते. Elephants are not afraid of [the] barking [of] dogs.

§ 398. The oblique infinitive + में also corresponds to an adverbial phrase:

हमें आने में कुछ देर हो गई. We arrived somewhat late.

भारत में किसान आग जलाने में गोबर इस्तेमाल करते हैं.
In India the peasants use cow-dung to make a fire.

§ 399. The oblique infinitive + the genitive-markers का, की, के :

यह कमरा सोने का है. This is a bedroom (lit. a room for sleeping).

क्या यह पीने का पानी है?	Is this drinking water?
उस ने हिन्दी सीखने की कोशिश की.	He tried to learn Hindī.

§ 400. The oblique infinitive + का (की, के) + negation expresses unwillingness or inability to perform the action:

वह वहाँ जाने का नहीं.	He won't go there.
मैं यह काम नहीं करने का.	I (masc.) can not do this work.
मैं यह कभी नहीं मानने की.	I (fem.) will never consent to this.

§ 401. The adjectives योग्य, लायक, क़ाबिल "suitable, worth" use the oblique infinitive with our without के:

यह मन्दिर देखने (के) योग्य है.	This temple is worth seeing.

§ 402. Oblique infinitive without postposition is used with लगना, देना and पाना. See under the respective combined verb § 420.

INVARIABLE AND GN-MARKED INFINITIVES.

§ 403. Infinitive followed by the verbs होना, पड़ना and चाहिये expresses an obligation. The infinitive is usually invariable in –ग्रा:

मुझे जाना है.	I have to go.
मुझे जाना पड़ता है.	I have to go.
मुझे जाना चाहिये.	I must go.
विद्यार्थी को पढ़ना चाहिये.	A student should study.
उसे गाड़ी से उतरना ही पड़ा.	He had to get off the train.
मोती को स्टेशन तक सामान लेकर जाना पड़ा.	Motī had to go to the station with the luggage.

§ 404. If the infinitive has a direct object it can either remain invariable masc. sing. in –ग्रा or agree with the object in gender and number, as do the finite verbs होना and पड़ना. चाहिये, however, is invariable in Standard Hindī.

मुझे ग्रपने दोस्तों को चिट्ठियाँ लिखनी हैं.	I have to write letters to my friends.

माली को लकड़ी काटनी है। The gardener has to cut wood.

गाँव के बाहर ही मुझे अपनी गाड़ी खड़ी कर देनी पड़ी। I had to park my car right outside the village.

उसे रोज़ ग्वाले के यहाँ से दूध लाना होता था। He had to bring milk every day from the milkman's house.

धोबी को कपड़े फिर साफ़ करने पड़े। The washerman had to wash the clothes again.

मोहन को जुर्माना देना पड़ेगा। Mohan will have to pay a fine.

पीने का पानी साफ होना चाहिये। Drinking water should be clean.

दूसरों की बात सुननी चाहिये। One should listen to others.

कसम कभी नहीं खानी चाहिये। One should never swear [by anything].

§ 405. However, some speakers use the invariable infinitive:

औरत को इसी दुकान से सब्ज़ी खरीदना चाहिये। The woman should buy vegetables from this store.

हम को अपनी किताबें लाना था। We had to bring our own books.

THE ABSOLUTIVE.

§ 406. The SHORT ABSOLUTIVE looks identical to the stem: चल, देख, सुन. This form of the absolutive is found as first member in combined verbs (see § 418) and in poetry.

§ 407. The common type of absolutive is formed by adding the INVARIABLE suffix -कर to the stem, written as one word or as two: चलकर, देखकर, आ कर, जा कर.

§ 408. Absolutives may also be formed by adding the suffix -के, or करके to the verbal stem: चलके, देखके, चल करके, देख करके.

§ 409. The absolutive-marker -कर is identical to the stem of the verb करना. Therefore, for reasons of euphony, the absolutive of करना is करके.

§ 410. If two verbal stems are juxtaposed, the absolutive-marker is added only to the last verb: खा-पीकर, रो-रोकर.

§ 411. The absolutive is a NON-FINITE verbal form. It gets its temporal value from the finite verb of the clause. The absolutive usually has the same subject as the finite verb, but sometimes the absolutive is used more loosely. The absolutive describes an action which either precedes the action expressed in the finite verb or is simultaneous with it according to the context.

§ 412. The Hindi sentence tends to avoid more than one finite verb, so accompanying or preceding actions are delimited by an absolutive. As a verbal form the absolutive can have the same kind of extensions as the finite verb, i.e. direct/indirect object, adverbs, etc. The most convenient way to render an absolutive into English is to coordinate it with the finite verb, adding "and" (see SYNTAX § 479):

मैं सोचकर कह दूँगा.	I'll think it over and tell you.
एक लाल रंग की साड़ी निकाल कर उस ने पहन ली.	She took out a red saree and put it on.
क्या आप वहाँ से शादी करके लौटेंगे?	Will you return from there after [your] wedding?
वह हिम्मत करके सुधा के पास बैठ गया.	He got up his courage and sat down next to Sudhā.

§ 413. Many absolutives can be rendered as adverbs, usually adverbs of manner:

वह दौड़कर आया.	He came running.
छाया ने सिर हिलाकर कहा.	Shaking her head Chāyā said.
खुश होकर बोली.	She said happily.
मोहन ने चौंक कर आँखें खोलीं.	Surprised, Mohan opened his eyes.

§ 414. Many absolutives have lost their verbal meaning and have acquired special meanings:

लेकर	with (lit. having taken, taking)
से लेकर	from

एक एक करके	one by one
बहुत करके	usually, too often
(से) होकर	via
रह रहकर	intermittently, at intervals
मिलकर	together
छोड़ कर	except
(से) बढ़ कर	better than, more than, superior
कपड़े लेकर वह नीचे आई.	She came down with the clothes.
औरतें एक एक करके चली गईं.	The women went away one by one.
वह बम्बई होकर यहाँ आया.	He came here via Bombay.
सबेरे से लेकर शाम तक वह पढ़ता रहा.	He kept studying from morning to night.
माँ से बढ़कर कोई गुरु नहीं.	There is no better teacher than mother.

COMBINED VERBS.

§ 415. By the term "combined verb" we mean two verbs, each used independently with its own distinct meaning, which combined with each other form a UNIT in which the first verb carries the semantic content and the second verb loses its independent semantic content and serves as an AUXILIARY to the main (i.e. first) verb. Example: the verbs खाना "to eat" and लेना "to take":

उस ने किताब ली.	He took the book.
उस ने खाना खाया.	He ate (food).
उस ने खाना खा लिया.	He ate (food).

In the last example लेना loses its independent meaning "to take" and serves uniquely as an auxiliary to खाना "to eat". However, लेना gives another nuance to खाना, in this case it conveys the idea that the action is directed towards the subject. (See लेना **1**, § 420.)

§ 416. If an object-taking verb has a non-object-taking verb as an auxiliary subjective construction is generally (but not always) used in the perfective aspect:

उस ने सब खोया.	He lost everything.
वह बैठा है.	He is sitting.
वह सब खो बैठा.	He lost everything.

In the last example **बैठना** as an auxiliary implies that the action was done through carelessness, etc. (see **बैठना 1** § 420), and the meaning "to sit (down)" is no longer present.

AUXILIARY VERBS.

§ 417. Auxiliary verbs can be divided into the following categories:

1. The grammatical function markers **जाना 3** and **रहना 1** are used to create the passive voice (see §§ 368 ff.) and the progressive-continuous aspect (see §§ 297, 317 ff.) respectively.

2. The modal auxiliaries **चाहना 1**, **सकना**, **पाना 1**, **2**, and **देना 2**.

3. The completive and/or intensifying auxiliaries **आना 1**, **3**, **उठना**, **खड़ा होना**, **घुसना**, **चलना**, **चुकना**, **जाना 1, 2, 4**, **5**, **डालना 1**, **2**, **देना 1**, **3**, **निकलना**, **निकालना**, **पड़ना 1**, **पहुँचना**, **बैठना 1**, **2**, **मरना**, **मारना**, **रखना**, **लगना 1**, **लाना**, **लेना 1**, **2**.

4. The inchoative auxiliaries **चलना** and **लगना 2**.

5. The frequentative-iterative auxiliary **करना**.

6. The continuative auxiliaries **आना 2**, **जाना 2**, and **रहना 2**, **3**, **4**.

7. The obligative auxiliaries **चाहिये**, **पड़ना 2**, and **होना**.

§ 418. The main, i.e. first, verb in a verbal combination will occur in one of the following forms:

1. Short absolutive (see § 406). This constitutes the largest group. As auxiliary verbs we find **आना 1**, **उठना**, **खड़ा होना**, **घुसना**, **चलना**, **चुकना**, **जाना 1**, **डालना 1**, **देना 1**, **निकलना**, **निकालना**, **पड़ना 1**, **पहुँचना**, **बैठना 1**, **मरना**, **मारना**, **रखना**, **रहना 1**, **लगना 1**, **लाना**, **लेना 1**, **सकना**.

2. a) Direct, sometimes GN-marked, infinitive: **चाहना 1**, **चाहिये**, **पड़ना 2**, and **होना**.

b) Oblique invariable infinitive in **-ए**: **देना 2**, **पाना 2**, **लगना 2**.

3. a) GN-marked imperfective participle: **आना 2**, **जाना 2**, **रहना 2**.
   b) Invariable oblique imperfective participle in -ए: **बनना 1**.
4. a) GN-marked perfective participle: **आना 3**, **जाना 3**, **4**, **रहना 3**.
   b) Invariable perfective participle in -आ: **करना**, **चाहना 2**.
   c) Invariable oblique perfective participle in -ए: **जाना 5**, **डालना 2**, **देना 3**, **बनना 2**, **बैठना 2**, **रहना 4**, **लेना 2**.

§ 419. The previously mentioned auxiliaries which are treated in more detail on the following pages do not form an exhaustive list. Many other verbs may occur as auxiliaries in verbal combinations. There seems to be a tendency in modern Hindī to increase the current stock of auxiliaries. The increase is based on one of the following principles:

1. Synonymity to the main verb as in आ पहुँचना (आना + पहुँचना), कह सुनाना (कहना + सुनाना), etc.
2. Antonymity to the main verb as in आ जाना (आना + जाना), उठ बैठना (उठना + बैठना), भाग खड़ा होना (भागना + खड़ा होना), etc.
3. Synonymity to already existing and frequently used auxiliaries: along with जाना "go" we also find चलना, घुसना, निकलना, etc.

Consequently, the following alphabetical list is not exhaustive.

§ 420. COMMON AUXILIARY VERBS .

आना 1 (अ) "to come"

The short absolutive + आना basically serves as a completive. It is common with verbs of motion.

फिर एक दिन बिना सूचना दिए लौट आए.
Then one day [you] returned without notice.

इस कोशिश में उन की आँखों में आँसू निकल आते.
Tears would come into their eyes in this attempt.

शाम को वह लण्डन पहुँच आया. He arrived in London in the evening.

Note the expression हो ग्राना "to become:

उस की ग्राँखें कुछ गिली हो ग्राईं.	Her eyes became somewhat moist. (Compare हो जाना which is more frequently used.)

ग्राना 2

GN-marked imperfective participle + ग्राना underlines that the action is continuous :

हम सालों से यहाँ रहते ग्राए हैं.	We have lived here for years.
ग्ररथी बढ़ती ग्रा रही है.	The bier is proceeding [steadily].

ग्राना 3

GN-marked perfective participle + ग्राना implies that the action expresses the immediacy of the action:

शत्रु चढ़ा ग्राता है.	The enemy is advancing.
बादल घिरे ग्राते हैं.	Clouds are gathering.

Note the expression चला ग्राना "to come":

एक ग्रपरिचित व्यक्ति उसे लेने के लिए चला ग्राया था.

An unknown person had come to take him.

Cf. चला जाना "to go away".

उठना (ग्र) "to rise, to get up"

Short absolutive + उठना indicates that the action happens suddenly. It is often combined with non-object-taking verbs.

एकाएक छाया चीख उठीं.	Suddenly Chāyā screamed out.
बच्चा रो उठा.	The child burst into tears.
हम भय से काँप उठे.	We shuddered with fear.
ठहाके से सारा कमरा गूँज उठा.	The whole room resounded with a [sudden] laughter.

करना (स) "to do"

Invariable perfective participle in -ग्रा + करना indicates that the action happens often and/or regularly.

दादी कहा करती थी कि...	Grandma used to say ...

नवंमबर में यहाँ वर्षा बहुत हुआ करती है.	It usually rains a lot here in November.
आप भी क्लब जाया कीजिए.	You also please come to the club [regularly].
वे तीनों रोज़ गपशप किया करते थे.	The three of them used to chit-chat every day.

खड़ा होना (अ) "to stand, to be standing'

खड़ा होना functions as a second member in a few combinations where it emphasizes the semantic content of the first verb by being antithetic to it. खड़ा होना may also convey the idea of permanence:

मेरे और इस खरगोश के बीच एक छोटा-सा झगड़ा उठ खड़ा हुआ है.	A little dispute has arisen between myself and this rabbit.
उस ने मुझे शनाख्त के लिए रोकना चाहा तो मैं भाग खड़ा हुआ.	When he wanted to stop me for identification I fled.

घुसना (अ) "to enter"

घुसना usually serves as an intensifying auxiliary to the short absolutives आ and जा.

वह चुपचाप रसोई में जा घुसी.	Silently she went into the kitchen.
वह मेरे कमरे में आ घुसा.	He came into my room.

चलना (अ) "to go"

Short absolutive + चलना implies the beginning of an action:

रातें लम्बी हो चलीं.	The nights began to be long.
यहाँ से लौट चलना चाहिए.	We have to start leaving from here.
उस के माथे से खून बह चला.	Blood began to flow from his head.
बगुले उड़ चले.	The herons flew off.

चाहना 1 (स) "to wish, to want"

Invariable infinitive + चाहना serves as a modality: to want to do V:

मैं जाना चाहता हूँ.	I want to go.
वह खाना खाना चाहता है.	He wants to eat.

चाहना 2

Invariable perfective participle in -आ + चाहना indicates that the action is immediately about to happen:

वर्षा आया चाहती है.	The monsoon is about to break.
लड़की बाहर जाया चाहती है.	The girl is about to go out.

चाहिए (see §§ 403-405).

चुकना (अ) "to finish"

Short absolutive + चुकना indicates that the action is completed:

हम सुन चुके हैं.	We have already heard [it].
उसे जो कुछ चुनना था वह चुन चुकी है.	Whatever she had to choose she has already chosen.
मैं खा चुका हूँ.	I have already eaten.
इस समय तक फसलें कट चुकी होती हैं.	At this time the harvest has already been cut.

Short absolutive + चुकना is the only possibility to express the **future perfect** in Hindī; the perfective participle + होगा is used as perfective presumptive (see § 355):

जब खाना खा चुकूँगा बाग में जाऊँगा.	When I have finished eating I shall go out in the garden.
कल तक मैं यह काम कर चुकूँगा.	I shall have finished this work by tomorrow.

जाना 1 (अ) "to go"

Short absolutive + जाना indicates the completion of the action.

वह सब दूध पी गया.	He drank up all the milk.
बाहर इसे कोई बिल्ली खा जाएगी.	Outside some cat will eat it (i.e. the bird) up.

जाना is especially common with verbs of motion:

वह बस से टकरा गया.	He collided with a bus.
थोड़ी देर बाद उसे होश आ गया.	After a little while she regained consciousness.
रहेगा या आज ही लौट जाएगा.	Will he stay or return already today?

जाना is often used to make a simple stative verb dynamic:

होना	to be	हो जाना	to become
सोना	to sleep	सो जाना	to go to sleep, to fall asleep
थकना	to be tired	थक जाना	to get tired

दो मिनट में वह सो गया.	He fell asleep within two minutes.
इतने काम से वह थक गया.	He got tired from so much work.
वह बहुत प्रसिद्ध हो जाएगी.	She will become very famous.

Note the idiom हो गया "it is finished, done".

जाना 2

GN-marked imperfective participle + जाना underlines that the action continues for a longer time:

वह चलता गया. He kept on walking.
रोग बढ़ता जाता है. The disease is steadily getting worse.
दिन दिन वह अधिक विवर्ण और पारदर्शी होती जाती है.
She is getting more pale and transparent day by day.
रात्रि का अन्धकार धीरे धीरे चारों ओर फैलता जा रहा था.
The darkness of the night was slowly spreading all around.

जाना 3

GN-marked perfective participle + जाना is used to form passive voice. See §§ 368-376.

जाना 4

GN-marked perfective participle + जाना can also be intensifying without any passive meaning:

मैं दर्द से मरा जा रहा हूँ. I am dying of pain!
बर्फ़ पिघली जाती है. The ice is melting.

अपने दोस्त को मरने के लिए यहाँ क्यों छोड़े जाते हो?
Why do you leave your friend here to die?

[cf. जाना 5]

The compound चला जाना "to go away" is so common that it has lost its intensifying meaning:

वह चला गया. — He went away.
चले जाओ! — Go away!

जाना 5

Invariable oblique perfective participle in -ए + जाना is either intensifying or indicates a continuous action:

जब तक मुझ में शक्ति है मैं काम किए जाऊँगा.
I shall continue to work as long as I have strength in me.

कहे जाओ! — Keep on talking!
कुत्ता भूँके जा रहा था. — The dog kept on barking.
अपने दोस्त को मरने के लिए यहाँ क्यों छोड़े जाते हो?
Why do you leave your friend here to die?
पानी बरसे जा रहा था. — It was raining continuously.

डालना 1 (स) "to throw"

Short absolutive + डालना implies that the action is carried out emphatically or violently. It is usually combined with object-taking verbs.

बच्चे ने शीशा तोड़ डाला. — The child smashed the mirror.
उस ने अपने भाई को मार डाला. — He beat up his brother.
जो कुछ बाकी है उसे भी कह डालिए!
Whatever is left [to say], out with that too!
छाया ने झाड़ू काकी के हाथ से ले ली और स्वयं सफ़ाई कर डाली.
Chāyā took the broom from her aunt's hand and swept [the room] clean herself.

डालना 2

Invariable oblique perfective participle in -ए + डालना gives the same nuance as with डालना **1**.

मुझे बचाओ यह मुझे मारे डालता है.	Save me, he is going to kill me!

देना **1** (स) "to give"

Short absolutive + देना completes and rounds off the action. It also indicates that the action is directed to the object. (Cf. लेना **1**).

माँ ने बच्चे को खाना खिला दिया.	The mother fed the child.
उस ने घर छोड़ दिया.	He left home.
ठाकुर ने सहमति दे दी.	The landlord gave [his] consent.
उस ने किताब अलमारी में रख दी.	He put the book in the bookcase.

When देना is combined with non-object-taking verbs the subjective construction is used:

बच्चा रो दिया.	The child burst into tears.
सुधा घर की ओर चल दी.	Sudhā set off towards home.

देना 2

Combined with oblique infinitive + देना means "allow, give permission to":

मुझे जाने दो.	Let me go!
मेरे पिता जी मुझे सिगरेट पीने नहीं देते.	My father does not allow me to smoke.
जो जी में आए उसे करने दो.	Let him do what he fancies.

देना 3

Invariable oblique perfective participle in -ए + देना puts emphasis on the action:

मैं कहे देता हूँ...	That I say ...
अभी रोटी पकाए दे रही हूँ.	I'll make the *roṭīs* right away.

निकलना (अ) "to come out, emerge"

Short absolutive + निकलना indicates that the action takes place suddenly and unexpectedly, or that it will come out well.

मेरा दोस्त इधर आ निकला.	My friend happened to come here.
इस मौके पर मेरे नए जूते चरमरा निकले.	On this occasion my new shoes happened to squeak.
मेरा व्यापार चल निकलेगा.	My business will succeed.
तीन लोग किसी तरह जान बचाकर भाग निकले.	Three people somehow managed to save their life and flee.

निकालना (स) "to extract"

Short absolutive + निकालना indicates that the action is successful:

राजपाल ने किताब ढूँढ़ निकाली.	Rājpāl found the book [having looked for it].
पुलिस चोर को खोज निकालेगी.	The police will find the thief [having searched for him].
आखिर उस ने एक तरकीब सोच ही निकाली.	Finally he thought out a device.

पड़ना 1 (अ) "to fall"

Short absolutive + पड़ना indicates that the action happens suddenly and unexpectedly:

गाड़ी चल पड़ी.	The train set off.
योगी पागल सा नदी में कूद पड़ा.	The yogī, like a madman, jumped into the river.
बच्चा पेड़ से गिर पड़ा.	The child tumbled down from the tree.

पड़ना 2

See Infinitive §§ 403-405.

पाना 1 (स) "to get, to obtain"

Short absolutive + पाना is used as a modal verb "to be able to, succeed, to get the opportunity to". The ability to act depends on exterior circumstances. Cf. सकना.

वह शाम तक नहीं ग्रा पाएगा. — He will not be able to come until the evening.

बहुत कठिनता से वह ग्रपने को संभाल पाता. — He managed to pull himself together with great difficulty.

वह चाहते हुए भी नहीं खा पा रही थी. — She could not eat even if she had wanted to.

In tenses using the perfective aspect पाना commonly takes subjective construction, but objective or neutral construction may also be used:

मैं ग्रभी तक ग्राप की पुस्तक नहीं पढ़ पाई हूँ. — I have not been able to read your book yet.

मैं ग्रपना काम नहीं कर पाया. — I have not been able to do my work.

राम ने चिट्ठी न लिख पाई. — Rām could not write the letter.

पाना 2

Oblique infinitive + पाना have the same function as short absolutive + पाना.

Subjective construction is used in tenses with perfective aspect.

मैं बनारस नहीं जाने पाया क्योंकि मुझे इलाहाबाद में कुछ काम था. — I could not go to Benares, because I had some work [to do] in Allahabad.

मैं यह काम करने नहीं पाया. — I could not do this work.

तुम नहीं जाने पाग्रोगे. — You will not be able to go.

पहुँचना (ग्र) "to arrive"

पहुँचना is commonly used with the short absolutives ग्रा and जा to round off the action:

सीता जब कपड़ों को साबुन लगा चुकी तो ठाकुराइन आ पहुँची.
When Sītā had already put soap on the clothes the landlord's wife arrived.

बनना 1 (अ) "to be made"

Invariable oblique imperfective participle + बनना indicates that the action is possible or worth doing. The logical subject (or agent) takes the postposition से.

यह सब देखते ही बनता है. — All this is really worth seeing.
मुझ से वहाँ जाते नहीं बनता. — I cannot go there.

बनना 2

Invariable oblique perfective participle + बनना is used in the same way as बनना **1**:

मुझ से जाये नहीं बनता. — I cannot go.

बैठना 1 (अ) "to sit down"

Short absolutive + बैठना indicates that the action is carried out in a careless, negligent or dishonest way:

कॅंग्रेसजन देहाती जनता से संपर्क खो बैठे हैं.
The Congress people have lost contact with the rural population.
यह कुछ बदमाशी कर बैठे तो क्या करूँगी.
Should he commit some villainy, what shall I do?
उस ने यह सोसायटी बना ली और नेता बन बैठा.
He formed this society and became [its] leader.

However, in a sentence like वे लारी में जा बैठे the correct translation is obviously "They went and sat down in the lorry".

बैठना 2

Invariable oblique perfective participle in -ए + बैठना has the same meaning as बैठना **1**.

मरना (अ) "to die"

Short absolutive + मरना indicates disapproval and/or contempt:

हमें देखते ही कुत्ता भूँक मरता है. As soon as he sees us the [damned] dog barks.

तू रोज़ रोज़ अपना रोना लेकर हमारे यहाँ आ मरती है.
Every day you come to us and [bother us] with your snivelling.

आखिरकार तुम अपनी आदतों के गुलाम बन मरे.
Finally you have become a slave of your habits.

मुझे तङ्ग मत करो कहीं दूर जा मरो! Don't bother me, get lost!

मरना in combination with verbs implying death means simply "to die":

वह जल मरा. He burned to death.

वह डूब मरा. He drowned.

चलो भाई नदी में डूब मरो! Brother, go and drown yourself in the river!

मारना (स) "to beat, to kill"

Short absolutive + मारना has the same meaning as short absolutive + डालना, but is more emphatic. The combination can also express carelessness and/or thoughtlessness, disapproval or contempt:

उस ने एक ही धक्के से दरवाज़ा खोल मारा.
He shoved the door open with a single [hefty] push.

लड़कों ने सारा दिन गप्पों में बिता मारा.
The boys idled away the whole day gossiping.

उस ने बच्चों को भूतप्रेत की कहानियाँ सुना कर डरा मारा.
He terrified the children by telling them ghost-stories.

अंग्रेज़ी अखबारों में राजनैतिक लेख लिख मारा करते थे.
He used to scribble political articles in the English newspapers.

रखना 1 (स) "to put"

Short absolutive + रखना emphasizes the result of the action:

मैं ने एक जगह रोक रखी है.	I have reserved one seat.
सभी ने सफ़ेद कपड़े पहन रखे थे.	Everybody had dressed in white clothes.
उस ने सब्जी थाली में परोस कर उन के सामने ला रखी.	She put the vegetables on a *thālī* and put it down before him.

रखना 2

Invariable oblique perfective participle in -ए + रखना has the same meaning as रखना **1**.

रहना 1 (अ) "to live, be, remain"

Short absolutive + GN-marked perfective participle of रहना is used to form progressive-continuous aspect. See §§ 297, 317-320.

रहना 2

GN-marked imperfective participle + रहना indicates that the action continues over a certain period or is habitual:

वह सबेरे से शाम तक काम करता रहता है.	He keeps on working from morning to night.
पत्र भेजते रहो!	Keep on sending letters!
मैं अख़बार पढ़ता रहा.	I continued to read the paper.

The compound जाता रहना means "keep on going", but is also used idiomatically in the meaning " to disappear, lose, die":

उस की एक आँख जाती रही थी.	He had lost one eye.

रहना 3

GN-marked perfective participle + रहना emphasizes the continuity of the action:

उस पहाड़ की चोटी बर्फ़ से ढकी रहती है. — The top of that mountain stays covered with snow.

आखिरी बार बच्चा रात के नौ बजे तक रुका रह गया. — Last time the child had stayed on until nine o'clock at night.

लोगों के घरों में नई फ़सल का अनाज आ गया रहता है. — The grain of the new harvest keeps coming into people's houses.

रहना 4

Invariable oblique perfective participle in -ए + रहना is used in the same way as रहना **3**, but always with object-taking verbs:

वह कोट पहने रहता है.	He [usually] wears a coat.
वह सदा पिए रहता है.	He is always drunk.

लगना **1** (अ) "to attach to, cling to"

Short absolutive + लगना is often used with verbs of motion to indicate that the result of the action remains:

जहाज़ किनारे पर आ लगा है.	The ship has anchored at the shore.

लगना **2** (अ)

Oblique infinitive + लगना gives an inceptive meaning to the action "to begin to V". This compound always takes subjective construction in tenses using perfective aspect:

वह बोलने लगा.	He began to speak.
वे धर्ती पर बैठकर आलू खाने लगे.	They sat down on the ground and began to eat the potatoes.

लाना (अ) "to bring"

Short absolutive + लाना is one of the combinations where the second verb लाना keeps something of its own semantic significance of "to bring":

घीसू पेड़ पर चढ़कर लकड़ियाँ तोड़ लाता.
Ghīsū would climb a tree and break firewood [and bring it along].

दूसरों के खेतों से मटर या आलू उखड़ लाते.
They would dig up peas and potatoes from other peoples' fields.

दोनों आलू भुन रहे थे जो किसी की खेत से खोद लाए थे.
The two [of them] were roasting potatoes which they had dug up from somebody's field.

In all these examples the first verb could be interpreted as an independent absolutive (see §§ 411-412)

लेना **1** (स) "to take"

Short absolutive + लेना completes and rounds off the action and makes it subject-oriented (cf. देना **1**) :

तुम ने खा लिया? — Did you eat?
आप ने बहुत हिन्दी सीख ली. — You have learnt a lot of Hindī.
मैं ने उस का पता लिख लिया. — I wrote down his address.
आनन्द ने यह नया घर उस की अनुपस्थिति में बनवा लिया था.
Ānand had had this new house built in her absence.

In the idiomatic expressions हो लेना and साथ हो लेना subjective construction is used in tenses using perfective aspect:

बहुत हो लिया. — That's enough!
मैं उस का साथ हो लिया. — I accompanied him.

लेना **2**

Invariable oblique perfective participle in -ए + लेना carries the same meaning as लेना **1**, but is more emphatic:

वह सब खाना खाए लेता है. — He eats up all the food!

सकना (अ) "to be able to"

Short absolutive + सकना is primarily a modal verb meaning "to be able to". The ability to execute the action depends on the subject. Subjective construction is used in tenses using perfective aspect. Cf. **पाना 1** and **2**.

क्या वह आ सकेगा?	Will he be able to come?
मैं आप की मदद भूल नहीं सकता हूँ.	I can't forget your help.
मैं उत्तर नहीं दे सका.	I could not answer.
वह आलोक को वापस नहीं ला सकी.	She could not bring Ālok back.

होना (अ) " to be"

See Infinitive §§ 403-405.

THE SUFFIX -वाला.

§ 421. The suffix -वाला has a wide use in Hindī and fulfills several important functions. It may be added to oblique infinitives, nouns, adjectives, adverbs, pronouns, and even to entire clauses. It may be written separately from the word or clause it qualifies.

§ 422. -वाला behaves either a GN-marked adjective in -आ (see paradigm § 203) or as an independent noun following the 1st or 2nd declension respectively (see §§ 33-34).

§ 423. The oblique infinitive + -वाला is used in the following ways:

1. as an agent noun, that is "one who does something" as in देखनेवाला "one who sees", i.e. a spectator, लिखनेवाला "one who writes", i.e. a writer, खेलनेवाला "one who plays", i.e. a player, बोलनेवाला "one who talks" i.e. a talker/speaker:

खिलौने रह गये, खेलनेवाला चला गया.	The toys remained, the player left.
खरबूज़ों को बेचने वाली रो रही थी.	The watermelon seller (fem.) was weeping.
यहाँ लोग अपने पड़ोस में रहनेवालों को ही नहीं जानते.	Here people don't even know those who live in their own neighbourhood.

2. as a part of the predicate expressing intention: जानेवाला "prepared to go, about to go", बोलनेवाला "about to talk" :

मैं दिल्ली जानेवाला हूँ.	I am about to go to Delhi.
गाड़ी छूटनेवाली है.	The train is about to leave.
जाने क्या होनेवाला था.	God knows what was about to happen.
मैं यह किताब पढ़नेवाली हूँ.	I am about to read this book.

3. A main clause containing the emphatic particle ही placed between the oblique infinitive and the suffix -वाला followed by a subordinate temporal clause introduced by कि describes that something was about to happen when something else happened:

मैं उत्तर देने ही वाली थी कि दरवाज़ा खुल गया.
I was about to answer when the door opened.

वह बाहर जाने ही वाला था कि उस के पिता जी मर गए.
He was about to go abroad when his father died.

मैं तुम्हें चिट्ठी लिखने ही वाला था कि उस का तार आया.
I was about to write you a letter when his telegram arrived.

4. The oblique infinitive + -वाला can be used as an adjectival modifyer:

वह हिन्दी सीखनेवाला विद्यार्थी है. He is a student of Hindī.

भूत-प्रेत की या दूसरी डरानेवाली कहानियाँ बच्चों को मत सुनाओ.
Don't tell ghost-stories or other frightening stories to the children!

§ 424. Added to nouns, which always are in the oblique form, -वाला indicates profession, place of origin or residence, a temporary or permanent characteristic etc. as in दूधवाला "milkman", बिजलीवाला "electrician", बसवाला "bus-driver", गाँववाला "villager", आगरेवाला "man from (or living in) Āgrā", बड़ी नाक वाली "a woman with a big nose", सफ़ेद कुरतेवाला "a man in a white kurtā", etc. A subjacent oblique infinitive can be implied: दूध (बेचने)वाला, गाँव (में रहने)वाला, सफ़ेद कुरता (पहनने)वाला.

क्या दूधवाला आ रहा है? Is the milkman coming?

गाँववाले कभी शहर आते हैं. The villagers sometimes come to the city.

बड़ी नाक वाला बाहर गली में खड़ा हुआ था.
The man with the big nose was standing outside in the lane.

§ 425. -वाला can be added to adjectives – which always are in the oblique form – or to adverbs:

उस को पीलेवाली साड़ी चाहिये. She wants the yellow saree.

मैं सब से नीचेवाला कपड़ा चाहता हूँ.
I want the cloth which is lying furthest below.

वह ऊपरवाले कमरे में काम करता है. He is working in the room above.
बीच वाली चटाई पर कमालिये वाली और उस का लड़का है.
The woman from Kamāliyā and her lad are on the carpet in the middle.

§ 426. -वाला added to nouns or entire clauses renders what precedes into a modifying adjective as in

मुझे पन्द्रह दो रुपये वाली टिकटें चाहिये.
I want fifteen two rupee stamps.
वह चार बजे वाली गाड़ी से आता है.
He usually comes with the four o'clock train.

§ 427. A -वाला clause can substitute for a relative clause. Compare the following sentences:

जो औरत सब से पहले बोली थी उस ने विरोध किया.
सब से पहले बोलनेवाली ने विरोध किया.
She who had spoken first protested.
जो आदमी खेत पर काम कर रहा है, वह मेरा भाई है.
खेत पर काम करनेवाला आदमी मेरा भाई है.
The man who is working in the field is my brother.
जो पानी नदी से आता है, उसे मैं नहीं पी सकता.
नदी से आनेवाला पानी मैं नहीं पी सकता.
I cannot drink the water that comes from the river.

THE SUFFIX -सा.

§ 428. The GN-marked adjectival suffix -सा, -सी, -से may be added to adjectives, nouns, pronouns and verbs in the sense of "as, like, -ish, rather".

§ 429. With adjectives -सा implies that the quantity or quality changes somewhat:

साड़ी का रङ्ग लाल-सा था.	The saree had a reddish colour.
छोटी-सी लड़की दरवाज़े पर दिखाई दी.	A smallish girl appeared at the door.
थोड़ा-सा मक्खन दे दीजिए.	Please give [me] a little butter!

§ 430. A postposited -सा is used to express likeness and agrees in gender, number and case with whatever it modifies or is attributive to:

ऐसी बच्चों की सी बातें सुनना नहीं चाहता.	I don't want to hear this kind of childish talk.
एक पेड़ के नीचे दो आँखें सी चमक रही थीं.	Under one tree there was [something] like two eyes shining.
योगी पागल सा नदी में कूद पड़ा.	The yogī jumped in the river as if [he was] mad.
वह मर सा गया.	He seemed dead.

§ 431. In some cases -सा can be replaced by the pronominal adjective जैसा:

योगी पागल जैसा नदी में कूद पड़ा.	The yogī jumped in the river as if [he was] mad.

§ 432. Regarding the interrogative कौन-सा and कौन कौन-सा see §§ 163-164.

PARTICLES AND OTHER MARKERS.

§ 433. Particles are of the following kinds: 1. honorific, 2. affirmative and negative, 3. interrogative, and 4. emphatic.

§ 434. The honorific particle जी expresses respect and are commonly used together with names.

1. जी is placed after the name:

गान्धी जी कहते थे कि ...	Gāndhī used to say that...
क्या ग्राप यहाँ रहते हैं शर्मा जी?	Do you live here, Mister Śarmā?

§ 435. The common affirmative particle is हाँ "yes". It is often combined with the honorific particle जी, which usually precedes हाँ:

हाँ, नौकर ग्रा गया है.	Yes, the servant has come.
जी हाँ, मैं उन से कह दूँगी.	Yes, I'll tell them.

§ 436. The adverbs ज़रूर and ग्रवश्य "certainly", ठीक "right", and ग्रच्छा "fine" serve as affirmative particles.

§ 437. Of the three adverbs of negation (see § 227 C), only नहीं serves as negative particle "no". Like हाँ it may be preceded by जी:

नहीं, ऐसा नहीं हो सकता.	No, it can't be so.
क्या सीता ग्राई है – जी नहीं.	Has Sītā come? – No [sir].

§ 438. 1. The interrogative adverb क्या, if placed first in the sentence, functions uniquely as a question-marker and is left untranslated (see § 169):

क्या नौकर ग्राया है?	Has the servant come?

2. The interrogative adverb क्यों "why?" also introduces a question, but since it expresses a doubt and/or surprise, it may be translated as "what!" or "really":

क्यों तुम ने यह कहा ?	What! You said this?

§ 439. The three emphatic particles ही, भी and तो fill a variety of functions which cannot always be rendered into English. They are always placed **after** the word they emphasize.

§ 440. ही has basically an exclusive or restrictive sense. When it underlines that there is no alternative, it is often translated with "only":

हम लोग हिन्दी ही बोलते हैं.	We speak only Hindī.
ज़मीनदार ही वहाँ घुस सकते हैं.	Only the landlord can enter there.
वह पढ़ता ही था.	He only studied (i.e. and did nothing else).
मैं ने कपड़ा यहाँ ही खरीद लिया.	I bought the cloth right here.

For emphatic forms of demonstrative pronouns see § 117.
For ही + -वाला see § 423.3.
For imperfective participle + ही see § 384.

§ 441. भी is often inclusive and may be translated as "also" or "even":

मैं भी आया हूँ.	I also have come.
नौकर भी यह जानते हैं.	Even the servants know this.
उस गाँव में कुआँ भी नहीं था.	There wasn't even a well in that village.

For the use of भी with indefinite relative pronouns see § 200. 3.

§ 442. तो has the sense of "rather", "on the other hand". It is often has to be left untranslated in English. The emphatic तो has to be distinguished from the adverb तो / तब "then"(see §§ 452 and 458):

बात तो यह है कि...	It is rather so that ...
आप अच्छे तो हैं?	You are all right, aren't you?
यह तो बच गई.	She, for her part, escaped.

CONJUNCTIONS.

§ 443. There are two kinds of conjunctions: coordinating and subordinating.

COORDINATING CONJUNCTIONS.

§ 444. Copulative conjunctions coordinate words or phrases having the same syntactic function. The most common is ग्रौर "and":

जंगल में खरगोश ग्रौर कछुग्रा रहते थे.	In the jungle there lived a rabbit and a turtle.
वह बच्चों को फल ग्रौर मिठाई दे रहा था.	He was giving fruit and sweets to the children.
उस ने मुझे देखा ग्रौर कहा...	He saw me and said...

Note that Hindī usually avoids the coordination of finite verbs. See Absolutive §§ 411-412 and Syntax § 479.

§ 445. In formal discourse ग्रौर may be replaced by the *tatsam* तथा or एवम (which both mean "and" in Hindī):

महात्मा गान्धी ने सत्य एवम ग्रहिंसा दोनों का उपदेश दिया.	Mahātmā Gāndhī preached both truth and non-violence.

§ 446. Of the Persian conjunctions -ग्रो- and व "and", -ग्रो- is common in Urdū, whereas व has a somewhat wider use in Standard Hindī:

दिलोजान से	with heart and soul
ग्राबोहवा	climate (lit. water and air)
ग्रपना नाम व पता लिखिये.	Please write your name and address!

§ 447. Disjunctive conjunctions are या "or", ग्रथवा "or", या ...या "either ...or", न/नहीं ...न "neither ... nor", चाहे ...चाहे "whether ... or":

दो या तीन महीने बीत गये.	Two or three months passed.
तुम ने खाना खाया या नहीं?	Did you eat or not?

या तुम जाओ या मैं. Either you go or I.

मैं न तो घर जाऊँगा न मेरे भाई के घर.
I am neither going home nor to my brother's house.

चाहे तुम रहो चाहे जाओ... Whether you stay or you go...

§ 448. Adversative conjunctions are लेकिन, पर, परन्तु, किन्तु, मगर "but", and वरन, बल्कि "on the contrary, but also, rather":

मैं ने उस से पूछा लेकिन उस ने उत्तर नहीं दिया.
I asked him, but he did not answer.

वह किताब लाया ही नहीं बल्कि उस ने मुझे उसे पढ़ने में मदद दी.
Not only did he bring the book, but he [also] helped me to read it.

§ 449. Explicative conjunctions are इसलिए , emphatic इसीलिए "therefore, for this reason", and in more formal discourse अतेव, अतः "so, thus, therefore":

इसलिए मैं आया हूँ. Therefore I have come.

अतः इन सारे वक्तव्यों से निष्कर्ष निकलता है कि...
Therefore, from all these statements, the inference follows that...

All these conjunctions may be replaced by the locutions इस कारण (से), इस वजह से "for this reason".

SUBORDINATING CONJUNCTIONS.

§ 450. The most common conjunction to introduce a subordinate clause is कि "that":

खरगोश प्रसन्न था कि जज उस की रफ़्तार की प्रशंसा की.
The rabbit was pleased that the judge had praised his speed.

हर कोई यह जानता है कि वह बड़ा कमज़ोर है.
Everyone knows that he is very weak.

Note that कि often replaces जब "when" (cf. § 423.3).

§ 451. कि introduces direct speech, thoughts, and subjective considerations (see § 494):

उस ने मुझ से पूछा कि आप कैसे हैं? He asked me how I was doing.

उस ने कहा कि मैं सब कुछ बताऊँगा.
He said he would tell [it] all.

मैं ने सोचा कि मैं ज़रूर जाऊँगा. I thought that I would certainly go.

§ 452. Conditional clauses are introduced by अगर or यदि "if". The main sentence is introduced by an obligatory तो. The mood of the finite verb is chosen as follows:

1. if the action is considered certain, the present indicative, the simple past or the presumptive may be used. In these sentences the conjunction "if" may sometimes be replaced by जब "when".

अगर/जब बच्चा प्यासा है तो वह रोता है.
If/when the child is thirsty it weeps.

अगर/जब पिताजी वक्त पर वापस आते हैं तो हम आठ बजे खाना खाते हैं.
If/when father comes back on time we eat at eight o'clock.

अगर मैं वहाँ बीमार पड़ी तो डाक्टर के पास जाऊँगी.
If I fall ill there, I'll go to a doctor.

अगर मेहनत की तो सफल होगे. If you make an effort you will succeed.

अगर आप वक्त पर आएँगे तो हम वक्त पर खाना खा सकेंगे.
If you come on time, then we will be able to eat on time.

2. If the action is regarded as more or less uncertain, possible or desirable, the finite verb in the conditional clause will be in the subjunctive mood:

अगर खाना खराब हो तो आप बीमार हो जाएँ.
If the food is bad you may become ill.

अगर खाना खराब हो तो आप बीमार हो जाएँगे.
If the food is bad you will become ill.

अगर वह पकाए तो हम ज़रूर खाएँगे.
If he cooks we will certainly eat.

3. If the action is wholly hypothetical, the irreal is used (see § 340):

अगर मैं पढ़ सकता तो बहुत कुछ सीखता.
If I could read I would learn a great deal.

अगर धोबी अच्छा होता तो हम उस को धोने के लिए कपड़े देते.
If the washerman were good we would give him clothes to wash.

§ 453. In all the above examples अगर, जब and यदि may be deleted, but the presence of तो is obligatory:

बच्चा प्यासा है तो वह रोता है. If/when the child is thirsty it weeps.

मैं पढ़ सकता तो बहुत कुछ सीखता. If I could read I would learn a great deal.

धोबी अच्छा होता तो हम उस को धोने के लिए कपड़े देते.
If the washerman were good we would give him clothes to wash.

§ 454. Concessive clauses are introduced by the conjunctions अगरचे, हालाँकि and यद्यपि "although, even though", which correlate with फिर भी, तो भी, पर and लेकिन in the main clause. When यद्यपि is used, the correlative is usually तथापि:

अगरचे वह नाराज़ था, फिर भी हँसने लगा.
Although he was angry he began to laugh.

यद्यपि औद्योगिक विकास हो गया है, तथापि दरिद्रता रहेगी.
Even though there has been industrial development, poverty will remain.

§ 455. The subordinating conjunctions अगरचे, हालाँकि and यद्यपि can be left out, but the correlative must remain in the main clause:

गरीब होते हो, तो भी मैं तुम से प्रेम करती हूँ.
I love you even though you are poor.

§ 456. Causal clauses are introduced by the conjunctions चूँकि and क्योंकि "because, since, as". If the subordinate clause precedes the main clause, the latter is introduced by इस लिए :

चूँकि मेरे घर में बिजली नहीं है इस लिए मैं यहाँ आया हूँ.

Since there is no electricity in my house I have come here.

जानवरों के हृदय धड़कने लगे क्योंकि जज अब निर्णय सुनानेवाले थे.

The animals' hearts began to throb, because the judge was now about to announce the verdict.

§ 457. Final clauses are introduced by the conjunctions ताकि, कि and जिस से "so that, that". The subordinate clause is usually in the subjunctive mood:

मुझे पेंसिल दीजिए ताकि मैं आप का पता लिख सकूँ.

Please give me a pencil so that I can write down your address.

तारा कपड़ा लेकर बाहर गई जिस से वह उस का रङ्ग देखे.

Tārā took the cloth outside so that she could see its colour.

§ 458. Temporal clauses may be introduced by relative prominal adverbs. The temporal clause usually precedes the correlative clause which contains the corresponding demonstrative pronominal adverb (see table § 240). The most common is जब "when" and the correlative तब, तो "then":

जब मोहन दिल्ली आया तो उसे नौकरी नहीं मिली.

When Mohan came to Delhi he did not get a job.

जब बारिश होती है तो ज़मीन उपजाऊ हो जाती है.

When it rains the earth becomes fertile.

जब तक मैं ज़िन्दा रहूँगी तब तक लड़का यहाँ रहेगा.

The boy will stay here as long as I am alive.

जब से आप चले गए तब से मुझे नींद नहीं आती.

Since you went away I cannot sleep.

ज्यों ही मैं वहाँ पहुँचा त्यों ही काम शुरू किया.

As soon as I arrived there I began to work.

Another way to express "as soon as" is imperfective participle + ही (see § 384).

SYNTAX.

§ 459. The basic Hindī sentence structure is simple, but, as in any other language, a sentence can be expanded in various, seemingly complicated ways. Therefore it is very important to learn a technique to disentangle complex sentences. The first task is to discover the basic structure, and then fit in the various expansions of this basic structure. This can most easily be done by analysing the different syntagms (syntactic units) which make up a sentence. The nucleus of a sentence is the finite verb, which is normally found at the very end of the sentence (see § 464 below). Thereafter the subject, the direct object, the indirect object, and various adverbs are to be identified. Most Hindī syntagms are delimited by postpositions, which always serve as a point of reference. If a Hindī sentence is read at slow speed all the pauses will automatically fall at the end of each syntagm, i.e. just after the postposition. However, both the subject and the direct object may be in direct case (i.e. without postposition, see §§ 471A, 472, 474 below), so a pause has to fall after [the last member of] the subject or object.

§ 460. The sentence structure in subordinate clauses is exactly the same as in main clauses, so the method of analysis remains the same. For indirect speech see § 494 below.

§ 461. The **minimal** complete sentence in Hindī, as in English, consists of a subject and a verb:

लड़का देखता है.   The boy sees.

§ 462. The verb alone can constitute a complete sentence if the subject is inherent in the Person-Number marker as in the 1st person sing.:

देखूँ.   I may see.

§ 463. Obviously, in the imperative mood, the verb alone (simple or combined) can constitute the complete sentence:

जाइये Please go!   देखो Look!   हट जा Get lost!

§ 464. The normal word order in Hindī is **subject-object-verb**:

लड़का बिल्ली देख रहा है. The boy is looking at a cat.
लड़का अपनी बहिन को बुला रहा है. The boy is calling his sister.

§ 465. The indirect object precedes the direct object:

लड़का बिल्ली को चूहा दे रहा है. The boy gives a mouse to the cat.

§ 466. Adverbs of time are often at the beginning of a sentence before or just after the subject:

रात को लड़का बिल्ली को चूहा देता है.
At night the boy [usually] gives a mouse to the cat.

§ 467. Adverbs of space (location and direction) are inserted in the sentence before the verb:

वह यहाँ रहता है. He lives here.
मैं कल दिल्ली जा रहा हूँ. I am going to Delhi tomorrow.

§ 468. Adverbs of manner are inserted in the sentence before the verb and usually before the direct object:

वह बड़े आश्चर्य से मुझे देखता रहा. He kept looking at me with great astonishment.

§ 469. The word order can be changed for reasons of emphasis:

क्या किया तुम ने? What **did** you do?
उस से कभी नहीं बातचीत करूँगी. I'll never talk to **him**!

THE TECHNIQUE OF ANALYSING A HINDI SENTENCE.

§ 470. In all Hindi sentences, the **finite verb** has to be analysed **first**. Each finite verb contains either a P(erson)N(umber)-marker, an aspect-marker with G(ender)N(umber)-marker or a combination of these. The possibilities are as follows:

1. PN-marker only:
   a. the aspectless potential: जाऊँ, चलें, करे.
   b. the imperative mood: चल, करो, देखिये.
2. PN-marker + GN-marker:
   the aspectless presumptive: जाएगा, चलेंगी, करोगे.
3. Aspect-marker + GN-marker:
   a. the habitual past: चलता था, करती थी, देखते थे.
   b. the progressive past: चल रहा था, कर रही थी, देख रहे थे.
   c. the simple perfective: चला, देखा, किये, चलीं.
   d. the perfective past: चला था, की थी, देखे थे.
   e. the irreal in all aspects: चलता, करता होता, देख रहा होता, दखा होता.
4. Aspect-marker + GN-marker + PN-marker:
   a. the habitual present in indicative and subjunctive mood: चलता है/हो, करती है/हो, देखते हैं/हों.
   b. the progressive present in indicative and subjunctive mood: चल रहा है/हो, कर रही है/हो, देख रहे हैं/हों.
   c. the perfective present in indicative and subjunctive mood: चला है/हो, की है/हो, देखे हैं/हों.
   d. the presumptive in all aspects: चलता होगा, कर रही होगी, चले होंगे.

§ 471. Once the nature of the finite verb has been established, the **subject** has to be found. Its normal place is at the beginning of the sentence. The subject will be either in A. **direct case** or B. **oblique case** followed by the subject-marker ने :

A. If the subject is in direct case the finite verb agrees with it in gender, number and person. This is called subjective construction (see § 323), which is compulsory in all tenses, moods and aspects if the verb is non-object-taking (अकर्मक क्रिया), but which occurs only in imperfective and progressive aspects if the verb is object-taking (सकर्मक क्रिया):

वह देर से लौटा.	He returned late.
भारत स्वतंत्र हुआ.	India became independent.
वह साइकिल से उतरा.	He got off the bicycle.

आदमी हमेशा काम करता था. The man always worked.
लड़का बिल्ली देख रहा है. The boy is looking at a cat.

B. If the subject-marker ने (see § 80) occurs in the sentence, what immediately precedes (always in oblique case) **has to be the subject** and the **aspect** has to be **perfective** and the aspect-marked verb object-taking (सकर्मक क्रिया). The construction is either objective (see § 324) or neutral (see § 325).

1. Objective construction:
औरत ने केला खाया. The woman ate a banana.
मैं ने किताब पढ़ी है. I have read the book.
मोहन ने रास्ते पर साइकिल छोड़ दी. Mohan left the bicycle on the road.

2. Neutral construction:
मच्छरों ने उसे काटा होगा. The mosquitoes must have bitten him.
मैं ने औरत को देखा. I saw the woman.

§ 472. **Grammatical and logical subjects.**
In sentences describing physical or mental perceptions and experiences, the **logical subject** appears as an **indirect object** with the postposition को (see § 81.5), and the **grammatical subject** is in **direct case**. The verb in such sentences is always non-object-taking (अकर्मक क्रिया), and agrees with the grammatical subject. Consequently, the construction is always subjective (see § 323):

मुझ को बड़ी खुशी है. I am very happy.
(Lit. *Great happiness* is to me.)
उस को लज्जा आई. He/she felt ashamed.
(Lit. *Shame* came to him/her.)
मुझ को भूख लगती है. I am hungry.
(Lit. *Hunger* attaches to me)

§ 473. As pointed out earlier (see § 81.4 and §§ 403-405), the same phenomenon occurs in sentences expressing compulsion or necessity, i.e. constructions with infinitive + होना, पड़ना and चाहिये :

मुझ को जाना है. I have to go.
सीता को पेन्सिल चाहिये. Sītā needs a pencil.
उस को काम करना पड़ता है. He/she has to work.

§ 474. The next syntactic unit to be identified is **the direct object**. If present, it is to be found immediately before the finite verb. It is either in **direct case** (see § 66) or **marked by** the postposition को (see §§ 71, 81.1-2):

मोहन केले देता है.	Mohan gives *bananas*.
मोहन ने साइकिल छोड़ दी.	Mohan left *the bicycle*.
मैं ने बच्चों को देखा.	I saw *the children*.

§ 475. **The indirect object**, if present, is marked by the postposition को (see § 81.3) or in certain cases से (see §§ 83.2, 327). It signifies to whom or what the action is directed:

मोहन बन्दरों को केले देता है.	Mohan gives bananas *to the monkeys*.
पिता ने गाँववालों से बातचीत की.	Father talked *to the villagers*.
बन्दर बच्चे से खाना चुरा रहा है.	The monkey is stealing food *from the child*.

§ 476. After the finite verb, the subject and the object or objects have been identified, it remains to determine the circumstances for the action: when? where? and how? did it take place. In other words, adverbs of time, place and manner.
The following is a step by step illustration how a sentence is extended:

मोहन केले देता है. — Mohan gives *bananas* .
[केले = direct object]

मोहन बन्दरों को केले देता है. — Mohan gives bananas *to the monkeys*.
[बन्दरों को = indirect object]

मोहन सुबह बन्दरों को केले देता है. — Mohan gives bananas to the monkeys *in the morning*.

[सुबह = complement of time - answers the question **when?**]

मोहन सुबह मन्दिर में बन्दरों को केले देता है. — Mohan gives bananas to the monkeys *in the temple* in the morning.

[मन्दिर में = complement of place - answers the question **where?**]

मोहन सुबह मन्दिर में स्नेह से बन्दरों को केले देता है. — Mohan *lovingly* gives bananas to the monkeys in the temple in the morning.

[स्नेह से = complement of manner - answers the question **how?**]

§ 477. MODIFIERS.

Each basic syntactic unit illustrated above can be further expanded through modifiers which preceed the noun they modify.
There are four essential types of modifiers:

1. Adjectival modifiers: पुराना मन्दिर an old temple
2. Pronominal modifiers: वह लड़का that boy
3. Numeral modifiers: चार केले four bananas
4. Genitival modifiers: राम की गाड़ी Rām's car

For the suffix -वाला as modifier see § 426.

§ 478. Each element in the sentence analysed above can thus be expanded with one or more modifiers as for example:

हमारा छोटा मोहन	our little Mohan
सोलह पक्के पीले केले	sixteen ripe yellow bananas
उन सफ़ेद बन्दरों को	to those white monkeys
हर सुबह	every morning
नगर के पुराने मन्दिर में	in the city's old temple
बड़े स्नेह से	with great love. i.e. very lovingly

The sentence thus reads:
हर सुबह नगर के पुराने मन्दिर में हमारा छोटा मोहन बड़े स्नेह से उन सफ़ेद बन्दरों को सोलह पक्के पीले केले देता है.

Every morning our little Mohan very lovingly gives sixteen ripe yellow bananas to those white monkeys in the city's old temple.

COMPLEX SENTENCES.

§ 479. The most common way of extending a sentence is by replacing a finite verb with an **absolutive** (see §§ 411-412). Since the absolutive is a verbal form, it can govern all the elements which a finite verb can govern. The subject of the absolutive and the subject of the finite verb, however, is usually the same:

फ़िल्मों की सुन्दरियों को देखकर उन का दिल बल्लियों उछल पड़ता था.

Seeing the film-beauties his heart would skip a beat.

फ़िल्मों की सुन्दरियों को is the direct object to the absolutive देखकर, not to the finite verb.

वह फ़ौरन सौ रुपये देकर मेरी बकरियाँ खरीद लेगा.

He will quickly give [me] hundred rupees and buy my goats.

The dir. obj. सौ रुपये decidedly belongs to the absolutive देकर, but फ़ौरन can be interpreted as an the adverb of manner either to the absolutive or to the finite verb खरीद लेगा. Its place, however, makes it more likely to be the adverb of manner to देकर, not to the finite verb.

EXTENDED SENTENCES GOVERNED BY PARTICIPLES.

§ 480. Participles may assume an adjectival function as modifiers to nouns (see §§ 378-380). At the same time, being verbs, they can govern the same syntagm(s) as they would have governed as a finite verb.

1. कुछ दूर से उस ने बगीचे में खेलते (हुए) बच्चों को देखा.

From some distance he saw the children playing in the garden.

बगीचे में is the complement of place to the adjectival imperfective participle खेलते.

2. कुएँ के पास किताब पढ़ रहा लड़का बैठा था.

Near the well a boy was sitting reading a book.

किताब is the direct object to the adjectival progressive participle पढ़ रहा.

3. मेरी बुश्रा से लिखा (हुश्रा) पत्र कल रात को श्राया.

The letter, written by my aunt, came last night.

मेरी बुश्रा से is the agent of the adjectival past participle लिखा.

स्कूल में सीखी हुई हिन्दी की सहायता से बुढ़िया ने कहा.

With the help of Hindī learnt in school the old woman said…

स्कूल में is the complement of place to the adjectival past participle सीखी which modifies हिन्दी, not to the finite verb कहा.

§ 481. Let us consider in detail the following sentence:

उस रात जंगल में छिपी हुई गफ़ा से आए तीन आदमी अलिबाबा के घर के पास पहुँच गए.

That night three men, [who had] come from a cave hidden in the jungle, arrived at Alibābā's house.

The finite verb of the sentence is पहुँच गए, the subject is जंगल में छिपी हुई गफ़ा से आए तीन आदमी, but the basic sentence is

उस रात (तीन) आदमी (अलिबाबा के) घर के पास पहुँच गए.

That night (three) men arrived at (Alibābā's) house.

उस रात is an adverb of time and (अलिबाबा के) घर के पास an adverb of place to the main action expressed in the finite verb पहुँच गए.

In the original sentence the subject syntagm contains two participial modifiers, छिपी and आए, modifying गुफ़ा and आदमी respectively. These two participles can both be finite verbs in independent sentences:

1. जंगल में गुफ़ा छिपी हुई है. "There is a cave hidden in the jungle" ; and

2. उस गुफ़ा से तीन आदमी आए "Three men came from that cave", thus making it obvious that जंगल में must be the adverb of place to छिपी हुई गुफ़ा, and जंगल में छिपी हुई गुफ़ा in turn an adverb of place to आए.

EXTENDED SENTENCES GOVERNED BY INFINITIVES.

§ 482. As already stated, the infinitive is a verbal form which can govern direct objects, adverbs etc. exactly like a finite verb (see § 392). Also, as has earlier been stated (see §§ 393-402), infinitives + postposition function as equivalents to subordinate clauses. Further examples of this are:

इससे उसे छूने की पुलिस को हिम्मत नहीं हुई.

Therefore the police did not dare to touch him.

उसे "him" is the direct object to छूना which in the sentence above happens to be in oblique case since it is a genitival modifier to the noun हिम्मत "courage" .

भारत में किसान आग जलाने में गोबर इस्तेमाल करते हैं.

In India the peasants use cow dung to make a fire.

This sentence has two direct objects आग "fire" and गोबर "cow dung": आग is the direct object to the infinitive जलाना and गोबर is the direct object to the compound verb इस्तेमाल करना.

§ 483. To illustrate the complexity of a Hindī sentence and how to disentangle it consider the following sentence*:

मुंशी उल्फतराय के शराब के नशे में तिमंजिले से उड़ने की कोशिश करने पर वहाँ से गिरकर मर जाने की सूचना तार द्वारा जिस समय उन के एकमात्र सुपुत्र तथा उत्तराधिकारी मुंशी खुशबख्तराय उर्फ मिस्टर के० राय के पास आई उस समय वे एक एंग्लो-इण्डियन गर्ल के कारण एक टामी से पिटने के बाद अस्पताल से मरहम-पट्टी करवाकर अपने कमरे में दर्द से कराह रहे थे.*

* This sentence is taken from Bhagavatī Caraṇ Varmā's short story तिजारत का नया तरीका.

§ 484. In order to understand the structure of this long sentence the first task is to establish that we have a relative and a correlative clause, introduced by जिस समय "at which time" and उस समय "at that time" respectively. This implies that we will have to look for two finite verbs, one in the relative clause, the other in the correlative clause. They are found in their usual place at the end of the respective clauses: आई "came" is the finite verb in the relative clause. It immediately precedes उस समय which introduces the main (correlative) clause which in turn has the finite verb at the very end: कराह रहे थे "was (hon. pl., lit. were) moaning".

§ 485. Let us first concentrate on the relative clause.
The finite verb in the relative clause is आई is fem. sing. simple perfective of a non-object taking verb. Hence the subject must be fem. sing. in direct case. There are only two feminine nouns in the clause: कोशिश and सूचना. Of these कोशिश can be ruled out because it forms a compound verb together with the infinitive करना which moreover is in the oblique case followed by the postposition पर. Hence the subject must be सूचना "notice" which is further extended by the adverbial adjunct तार द्वारा "by telegram". So the basic sentence is:

जिस समय सूचना (तार द्वारा) आई
"at which time a notice came (by telegram)".

§ 486. सूचना is modified by मर जाने की "of passing away", so we learn that a notice of somebody's death came by telegram. Whose death? Here we are faced with a very clever economical use of language: the syntagm मुंशी उल्फतराय के "of Munshi Ulfat Rāy" is a genitival modifier to मर जाने की, but it also serves as modifier to another syntagm as we shall see below. के is masc. sing. oblique since मर जाने is in oblique case because of the following की.

§ 487. Having established the main sentence in the relative clause, we consider the postpositions in it: we find में, से, पर, द्वारा and के पास. Of these four पर is preceded by a verbal form, the oblique infinitive करने which is part of the compound verb कोशिश करना "to make an attempt, to try", while the other postpositions are preceded by nouns.

§ 488. The presence of an oblique infinitive + the postposition पर indicates that the clause is in fact equivalent to a temporal clause (see § 395.2). कोशिश "attempt" is modified by the oblique infinitive उड़ने की "of flying" (genitival modifier). तिमंजिले से "from the third floor" is an adverb of place to उड़ना whereas शराब के नशे में "in the intoxication of alcohol" is an adverb belonging to उड़ने की कोशिश करना "the attempt of flying". मुंशी उल्फतराय के "of Munshi Ulfat Rāy", finally, is a genitival modifier to उड़ना as well as to मर जाना (see above). के is masc. sing. oblique (see above) since उड़ने is in oblique case because of the following की. What we have here is actually an equivalent to a temporal clause

जब मुंशी उल्फतराय ने शराब के नशे में तिमंजिले से उड़ने की कोशिश की तो .... When Munshi Ulfat Rāy, intoxicated by booze (lit. "in the intoxication of alcohol"), tried to fly from the third floor, then ...

§ 489. The next clause is वहाँ से गिरकर "having fallen from there". वहाँ से obviously refers back to तिमंजिले से and is an adverb of place to the absolutive गिरकर which represents an action which precedes the infinitive मर जाना "to die". So, if we return to the temporal clause above, we could have a complete sentence as follows:

जब मुंशी उल्फतराय ने शराब के नशे में तिमंजिले से उड़ने की कोशिश की तो वे वहाँ से गिरकर मर गए. When Munshi Ulfat Rāy, intoxicated by booze (lit. "in the intoxication of alcohol"), tried to fly from the third floor, [then] he fell from there and died. (Regarding the coordination of the absolutive with the finite verb see above).

Note the stylistic refinement of the fact that, in the original sentence, मुंशी उल्फतराय के modifies मर जाना.

§ 490. As for the syntagm उन के एकमात्र सुपुत्र तथा उत्तराधिकारी मुंशी खुशबख्तराय उर्फ मिस्टर के० राय के पास "to his only beloved son and heir Munshi Khushbakht Rāy alias Mr. K. Rāy", the main word here is actually मुंशी खुशबख्तराय which has the apposition उर्फ मिस्टर के० राय "alias Mr. K. Rāy". This is contrary to the normal habit of putting the main noun or pronoun immediately before the postposition. उन के "his" is a genitival modifier to the main word, सुपुत्र तथा उत्तराधिकारी "beloved son and heir" are epithets to the main word, whereas एकमात्र "only" modifies सुपुत्र "only beloved son".

§ 491. In the main clause the finite verb is कराह रहे थे "was moaning" (masc. pl. progressive past, honorific plural). So the basic clauses are:

जिस समय (मुंशी उल्फतराय के मर जाने की) सूचना (तार द्वारा) मुंशी खुशबख्तराय के पास आई उस समय वे (अपने कमरे में दर्द से) कराह रहे थे.

At which time information (of the passing away of Munshi Ulfat Rāy) arrived (via telegram) to Munshi Khushbakht Rāy,
at that time he (i.e. Munshi Khushbakht Rāy) was moaning (with pain in his room).

§ 492. In the correlative clause there are two verbs besides the finite verb: the oblique infinitive पिटने in पिटने के बाद "after being beaten" (cf. § 396) and the absolutive करवाकर "having had done" with its direct object मरहम-पट्टी "bandage". Both the infinitive and the absolutive can be transformed into finite verbs in independent sentences:

मुंशी खुशबख़्तराय एक एंग्लो-इण्डियन गर्ल के कारण एक टामी से पिट गए.

Munshi Khushbakht Rāy got beaten up by a Tommy because of an Anglo-Indian girl.

(उन्हों ने) अस्पताल से मरहम-पट्टी करवाई.

He got [himself] bandaged in (lit. from) the hospital.

§ 493. In Varmā's sentence we learn in a concentrated form that the following events occured:

Munshi Ulfat Rāy was drunk. He tried to fly from the third floor. He fell down and died. A telegram arrived to his only beloved son and heir Munshi Khushbakht Rāy, alias Mr. K. Rāy, who, in turn, was moaning with pain in his room because he had been beaten up by a Tommy [in a fight] caused by an Anglo-Indian girl and he had had himself bandaged in the hospital.

§ 494. Hindī does not use indirect speech or discourse, but always uses the original direct speech, real or imaginary, preceded by the conjunction कि. The English translation, however, requires the use of indirect speech.

मैं ने कहा कि मैं अपने नौकर को ज़रूर भेज दूँगा.

I said that I would certainly send my servant.

The literal translation would be: "I said that I'll send my servant", in other words, despite the presence of कि, Hindi renders the speech as it would have been said in direct speech. This occurs with all verbs of saying, thinking, hearing, knowing, etc. :

मोहन ने सीता से कहा कि मैं तुम से प्यार करता हूँ.

Mohan said to Sītā that he loved her. (Lit. Mohan said to Sītā: "I love you".)

उस ने सोचा कि मेरी पत्नी वापस आएगी.

He thought that his wife would return.
(Lit. He thought: "My wife will return".)

उन के घर जाकर उन से कह दीजिए कि आप कल आइए.

Go to his house and tell him to come tomorrow.
(Lit. Having gone to his house please tell him: "You please come tomorrow".)

For the presence of कि see § 451.